DISNEY'S
AMERICA ON PARADE

DISNEY'S AMERICA

A HISTORY OF THE U.S.A.

Distributed by New American Library

ON PARADE

IN A DAZZLING, FUN-FILLED PAGEANT

TEXT BY DAVID JACOBS

Harry N. Abrams, Inc., Publishers, New York

LIBRARY OF CONGRESS CATALOGING IN PUBLICATION DATA

Jacobs, David, 1939-
    Disney's America on parade.

    Summary: Text, pictures, and photos record the
extravaganza of historical moments produced daily at
Disneyland and Walt Disney World to commemorate the
bicentennial during 1975 and 1976.
    Includes index.
    1. United States—History.   [1. United States—His-
tory]   I. Title. II. Title: America on parade.
E179.J32   973   75-22066
ISBN 0-8109-0510-8

Library of Congress Catalogue Card Number: 75-22066
Copyright © 1975 by Walt Disney Productions
Printed and bound in the United States of America
Printed web offset by Quad Graphics, Inc., Pewaukee, Wisconsin

CONTENTS

tensions with the British—The War of 1812—Florida, Texas, Oregon, and the idea of Manifest Destiny—The war with Mexico—From sea to sea—The Gold Rush—The Civil War—The engineering conquest of the nation.

3.
THE MAKING OF A PEOPLE

The first Americans: British, Dutch, French—Incentives for immigration—The Bill of Rights—The Industrial Revolution and the balance of trade—The first waves of immigrants: the Irish, the Germans, the Scandinavians—The trend toward imperialism—The Spanish-American War—The later waves: the East Europeans, the Italians, the Chinese, the Japanese, the Hispanics—the Afro-Americans after slavery.

4.
THE MAKING OF A SOCIETY

The pace of life in industrializing America—The train shrinks the nation—The beginnings of popular culture: vaudeville—The influence of Edison—Transportation and communication in the twentieth century—"America on Parade," a joyful birthday party for the Nation.

INTRODUCTION

Walt Disney's "America on Parade" is a celebration—a grand pageant honoring the United States of America on the occasion of its bicentennial anniversary. The heart of "America on Parade" is contained in a colorful procession conducted at Disneyland in Southern California and Walt Disney World in central Florida. Between June 1975 and September 1976 the pageant will unfold more than twelve hundred times and will be seen by an estimated twenty-five million people —probably the largest audience in history to witness a live theatrical production. In addition, books, records, and television presentations are spreading the spirit of the celebration, which the Disney organization refers to as a "birthday party for the country," to towns and cities throughout the nation.

Devised especially for this celebration, every element in "America on Parade" has been created in duplicate. Each parade consists of fifty units depicting milestones and important institutions in American history, from Columbus's discovery of the New World through the establishment of the government in Washington, D.C., to space exploration. In addition, the parade features more than one hundred and fifty doll-like characters representing the people of America.

Most of the parade units are more than twenty feet high— the highest is nearly thirty—and range from fifteen to forty feet in length; the characters are eight feet high. Beginning to end, the parade measures three-quarters of a mile and takes about half an hour to pass a given point. The size of the show makes the presentation easily visible. Visibility, however, is only one reason for the gigantic scale. For, like every aspect of the production, the bigness of the parade units and characters contributes to the celebratory atmosphere—an atmosphere calculated to make everyone, old as well as young, see the parade through the eyes of a child. To achieve this, the Disney organization designed the parade units to look like huge toys, and the characters to be outsized dolls.

Like all Disney projects, "America on Parade" began with research. For nearly a year researchers assembled information about America's history. Once the organization decided that a pageant would be the most suitable vehicle for its celebration, the Entertainment Division took charge. "America on Parade" was to be before all else a show—a big show, the biggest show that the Disney showmen had ever produced.

The first step was the selection of parade units, each a moving stage-and-set on which a significant milestone in American history could be dramatized. Some of the units symbolize specific events: Columbus's voyage, the making of the first American flag, the completion of the transcontinental railroad in Utah. For the most part, however, the planners concentrated on themes which, paraded in sequence, would capture the panorama of American achievements, population growth, and life-styles: a Pilgrim barn-raising characterizes colonial times; a flatboat and Conestoga wagon represent the young nation's mastery of the frontier; the automobile and airplane epitomize the revolution in transportation in the twentieth century; the pace and momentum of modern times are captured in units demonstrating the role of movies and television, "fast foods," and sports in everyday life. Thus "America on Parade" would be entertainment based on the nation's *social* history; it would tell the story, in song and dance, of the American people, what they have done, how they have lived, how they have changed.

Eventually the fifty parade units took shape on the drawing boards of Walt Disney Productions. Rough sketches became models; blueprints were made; motors were designed; the dimensions had to be adjusted to conform with the dimensions of Disneyland and Walt Disney World. When the blueprints and models were completed and checked for accuracy and practicality, the leading manufacturers of theatrical sets in cities throughout the country were commissioned to build the units. Always sticklers for detail and flawless craftsmanship, the Disney people had to be more particular than usual; for the units—manufactured, of course, in pairs, one unit for each park—would have to withstand the wear of daily and sometimes twice-daily parades.

For the most part the enormous animated figures on the great mobile stages are alike; the differences are drawn through costuming. Dressing the dolls proved to be one of the most complex problems that the pageant's planners faced. First, the costumes had to be accurate. Researchers and costumers had to work together to find appropriate fabrics, and to sew them as they would have been sewn fifty, a hundred, two hundred years ago. But that wasn't all: the material had to be bright enough to be seen clearly in the parade, tough enough to withstand the wear of six hundred outdoor performances, and practical enough to be cleaned quickly, easily, frequently. And if that didn't complicate things enough, there was the weight problem to worry about. For inside each of the eight-foot dolls would be a teen-age boy or girl who would have to perform with considerable energy under the very hot sun of Florida or California; therefore the fabric had to be lightweight. These diverse requirements notwithstanding, the costumers managed to locate an astonishing variety of fabrics that filled the bill.

Next the dolls were given appropriate wigs, hats, and props—all of which had to meet the same requirements met by the costumes.

American musical history provided researchers with more than enough songs for the parade, but the means to play those songs presented a problem. The planners wanted a band-organ sound, and two years before the start of the pageant they began a search for a real mechanical music box to play the selected songs. Eventually they found a beauty—a completely restored 1890 band organ—in Sikeston, Missouri. Known as "Sadie Mae," the instrument had some two hundred pipes and worked on the same principle as a player piano, except that punched-hole piano books were used instead of piano rolls. That was fine—except that the researchers discovered that only one man in the world was capable of making piano books by hand, and he was in Belgium. Determined to settle for nothing less than Sadie Mae, Disney sent the musical arrangements to Belgium and had the books made. Then Sadie Mae was taken apart and shipped to Nashville, where it was reconstructed in one of that city's many recording studios and given the new books to play. The tapes made in Nashville were sent to Los Angeles, where, in still another recording studio, Sadie Mae's music was embellished with the sounds of a moog synthesizer.

To make the most of the recorded music, the Disney engineers devised a system whereby selected units broadcast from their own loudspeakers while others broadcast their signals to radio receivers along the parade route; then the signals are rebroadcast through loudspeakers in fixed locations. The radio-transmitted signals and the signals broadcast from the units themselves are perfectly synchronized, and make music that is almost symphonic in its constancy and pacing.

At the conclusion of the parade, the recorded strains of Sadie Mae are mixed with melodies played by a live band. Inasmuch as each state in the union is honored during a specified week of the fifteen-month celebration, the Disney organization has invited marching bands—most of which are from high schools—to participate in "America on Parade."

"America on Parade" is presented once a day during the winter months, and twice a day during the summer months and on holidays. The second performance in the twice-a-day program is held at night, and is followed by an astonishing fireworks display. In their search for truly spectacular pyrotechnics, the Disney people spanned the globe—literally. The "Fantasy in the Sky" that concludes the Bicentennial celebration is the product of fireworks manufactured almost everywhere—the United States and Canada, Europe, and the Orient, including Korea, Taiwan, Japan, and the People's Republic of China.

A birthday party is what the Disney organization intended "America on Parade" to be, and a birthday party it is—though few birthday parties these days have so great a variety of guests. From the moment when the flag, fife, and drum come into view—carried by a trio of Revolutionary soldiers who look very much like Mickey, Goofy, and Donald—until the last, confetti-throwing parade unit—a circus train proclaiming America to be "the Greatest Show on Earth"—passes through the arched portal and out of sight, the atmosphere is unabashedly patriotic, joyful, proud. "We want people to go away with the feeling that they have really celebrated the Fourth of July," said one of the planners, "that they have really been to a party."

It is a party perfectly suited to the birthday of a two-hundred-year-old celebrant that still has a lot of the kid in it.

A NOTE ABOUT THE ILLUSTRATIONS

The historical text in this book is illustrated with photographs of maquettes and with drawings made by Walt Disney Productions in preparation for its Bicentennial pageant, "America on Parade." The maquettes are miniature models of the mobile units used in the parade, and the drawings are the designs for the costumes of the large animated figures which are the parade's main "performers."

Reproduced in the color foldout sections are photographs of the parade taken in June 1975 during the opening week of the pageant.

DISCOVERY AND SETTLEMENT

1.

DISCOVERY AND SETTLEMENT

WHEN, AFTER THIRTY-THREE DAYS AT SEA, Christopher Columbus sighted land in October, 1492, he called the islands he saw in his spyglass "Indies." When he stepped ashore on the twelfth of that month and found the islands populated, he called the natives who greeted him "Indians." As historian Samuel Eliot Morison has put it, Columbus thus made "one of the worst guesses in history."

Columbus's poor guesswork did not result from a flaw in his basic idea, but rather from a flaw in his basic mathematical assumption. Columbus's belief in a round world was not unique; it was not even unusual. That the Earth was a sphere had been known by educated people and by all but the most hardheaded seamen since the time of the ancient Greeks. What was not known was the size of the sphere. Columbus calculated that only about 2,500 miles separated the Canary Islands, off the west coast of Iberia, from the islands off the east coast of China. If that estimate were even close to correct, then a sea route westward from Europe to the Orient was altogether practical. Although the idea of such a route did not originate with him, Columbus was really its first serious and most persistent advocate in late fifteenth-century Europe.

Trade-routes had become the circulatory system of European economies. A commercial revolution had transformed European society during the previous two centuries. Commerce was the hub of the new society, and commerce meant trade. Trade required trade-routes, the most elusive of which connected the Mediterranean world with the Orient. Following the example of Marco Polo, European merchants sent expeditions overland to China. Some of the expeditions returned, years later, with the fine prod-

ucts of the Orient: spices, silks, carpets and other fine tapestry, porcelains, metals, gems, and so forth. But some of the expeditions did not return. The routes were treacherous, and the time, expense, and losses made the prices of Oriental goods prohibitively high. Therefore the young nations of Europe were eager to find a practical alternate route.

Throughout the fifteenth century, Portugal had been the most active European nation in exploration, and Columbus first proposed his idea of a westward route there. The Portuguese had been sending expeditions along the African coast, hoping to circumnavigate that continent, land on the Malabar coast, and enter China from the Indian subcontinent. Columbus explained that a due-west journey, entering China from its east coast, would be simpler, safer, and shorter. Although they listened attentively, the Portuguese decided to stick with their 'round-Africa approach. Next Columbus directed his campaign to Spain, whose commercial development had been lagging behind that of Portugal. After years of listening to the sales talk of the Genoese sailor, Ferdinand and Isabella supplied Columbus with three small ships, a crew, and their blessing, and hoped for the best.

Altogether Columbus made four round-trip voyages between Spain and the land he discovered, and though he saw miles

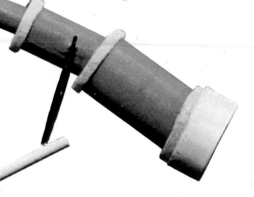

The kings of Portugal, England, and France all said no, but Queen Isabella of Spain, after at first refusing, reconsidered and gave Christopher Columbus what he asked for: ships, crews, and provisions for a voyage of discovery across the great "Western Ocean." Columbus was sure that he would find the east coast of Asia by heading west, but after more than two months at sea, his crew was in a near-mutinous mood. The ocean appeared endless, and the unknown terrors of the deep filled the men with horrible imaginings. On October 12, 1492, however, they saw land they called "the Indies." The voyagers had not in fact discovered a westward route to the Orient, but rather a prize much greater than anyone—including Columbus himself—could have imagined. They had discovered a New World.

and miles of diverse Caribbean shoreline (not, however, North America), and nothing to suggest the Orient, he probably never admitted that he had not in fact found Asian out-islands. Before his death, however, he did begin to speak of the lands as an "other World, whereby Spain . . . is to become the richest of all countries."

Christopher Columbus understood that this great mass of virgin land—"more land than there is in Africa and Europe," he wrote—could and would serve all humanity in a substantial, if not yet definable, way. In the wake of Columbus's discovery, the previously uncharted waters of the Atlantic Ocean became a highway between Europe and the New World.

Balboa and Magellan were committed to Christopher Columbus's original idea: finding a western trade route to the Orient. In 1513 Balboa led a small, hearty band of explorers through a Central American jungle in what is now Panama, and from a mountain peak they became the first Europeans to gaze out across the Pacific Ocean. Six years later, five ships under the command of Ferdinand Magellan left Seville to look for a westward sea route to the Orient. A Portuguese, Magellan had already sailed around Africa to Indonesia; knowing how treacher-

Columbus's crew was met on land by friendly natives. Impressed by the little gold trinkets some of the natives wore, the Europeans assumed that this New World held untold quantities of gold. The sailors searched from one island to the next, crossed mountains and valleys, confident that the gold was just beyond their reach, that they would find it tomorrow. Several generations of explorers and adventurers were infected by the same dream, and so the Europeans kept coming.

ous that route was, and hoping to find smoother sailing due west, he had convinced Spain to finance his trip. Arriving in the New World, Magellan, considered by many to be the greatest seaman who ever lived, sailed down the South American coast and discovered the almost unnavigable strait (now called the Strait of Magellan) through which he passed with great difficulty, emerging into the Pacific. Unaware of the vastness of the ocean, Magellan continued to sail west; days, weeks passed with no sign of land; supplies ran out, and some of the crew—in a mutinous mood, but too frightened to overthrow a man whose navigational skills were second to none—began to assuage their hunger by eating the leather chafing gear. Finally, in the fifteenth week following their passage through the straits, the expedition reached the island of Guam. After restocking, Magellan left Guam and landed ten days later in the Philippines, the Orient at last. Magellan's death during a native war in the Philippines prevented him from becoming the first sailor to encircle the Earth. Only one of the five ships Magellan had left with returned to Spain in 1522, but its cargo paid for the entire voyage.

By discovering the vastness of the Pacific Ocean, Magellan had helped to define the size of the globe—which was larger than many had previously calculated. Furthermore, while revealing that Columbus's assertion concerning a westward sea route was technically correct, the Magellan voyage at the same time rendered that assertion all but meaningless. The route was much too difficult and the distance much too long to be practical for trade. (The Portuguese 'round-Africa route was by far the more efficient, just as the Portuguese had suspected.) For the first time people could see the Earth as a sphere dominated by two enormous oceans and two great land-masses. On one side was the huge Eurasian mass and below it, Africa; on the other side, flanked by the oceans, were the two connected New World continents.

The Spanish explorers, for the most part, looked upon the Americas as repositories of wealth, wealth to be sought out, removed, and taken home. They were conquerors—*conquistadores*

—eager to collect the spoils of conquest. In most cases they were disappointed, with the exception of Cortés and Pizarro. Other Spaniards, convinced that the New World was filled with carefully hidden golden cities waiting to be looted, refused to give up the search. In the early 1540s, Coronado wandered throughout the lands known now as Arizona, New Mexico, Texas, Oklahoma, and Kansas, searching, searching. At the same time De Soto conducted the same search along the eastern coast of North America: Florida, Georgia, the Carolinas. Many of the Spanish wanderers confronted great wealth: the fertile soil of the Mississippi Valley; the Great Plains with all its bison; the deep, dense forests; the network of waterways that provided a natural transportation system through the wilderness. But this wealth was not wealth to the Spanish. Wealth was gold and silver, and since gold and silver had been found (though not nearly in the anticipated abundance) in Central and South America, the Spanish were less interested in colonizing North America than other European countries. They did establish a small colony in New Mexico, and claimed Florida, which its discoverer, Juan Ponce de Léon, believed contained the legendary Fountain of Youth. But for the most part the Spanish seemed oblivious to the real worth of the New World.

The Americas were literally a new world—not a series of Asian out-islands, not a gateway to someplace else, but a pair of large continents that would now be component parts in the larger world. Commerce—finance, manufacture, trade—was more than ever the lifeblood of European society. Other Europeans—mainly the English, French, and Dutch—evaluated the discovery of the New World differently. A New World to them meant new kinds of raw materials, new kinds of goods, new communities of growers and producers and consumers—a new marketplace in the ever-expanding world of trade. In their own way, of course, the second wave of Europeans was as much bent on exploiting the New World as the first wave had been. In time, several European countries established colonies in that New World.

Five years after Columbus first sighted his "Indies," another

Genoese sailor financed by a foreign monarch—in this case Henry VII of England—arrived in North America. His name was Giovanni Caboto, which he anglicized to John Cabot, and his route was very different from Columbus's. Cabot sailed far north in the Atlantic, possibly tracing the route of the very first Europeans to land in the Americas (the Norsemen, probably around the year 1000), and visited Labrador and Newfoundland in Canada. Like Columbus, Cabot thought he had reached an obscure part of eastern Asia.

In the 1500s, several British, French, and Portuguese expeditions explored the North Atlantic coastlines of the New World but found nothing to inspire settlement. They did, however, establish sea routes, and European fishermen were quick to take advantage of them. Fishing—mostly for cod—in the cold, shallow waters north of Cape Cod, they set up a small but far-flung network of makeshift shore stations along the coasts of what are now Maine, New Brunswick, Nova Scotia, and Newfoundland. Primitive though they were, these stations represented the earliest European settlements on the North American mainland.

In 1534 the French navigator Jacques Cartier discovered the St. Lawrence River and sailed up it, hoping that it crossed the continent all the way to the Pacific. It did not, and Cartier's venture stopped where Montreal now stands. Cartier's expedition, however, was followed by the inevitable fishermen, who made an important discovery of their own. The Indians who lived along the river wore handsome beaverskin capes. The Indians had an abundance of these skins and were willing to trade them for beads, knives, and other goods of European manufacture. When the French fishermen returned home, the handsome fur caused quite a sensation, and enterprising merchants sailed to the New World to acquire more. By the end of the sixteenth century the French fur trade was big business. The French established trading posts along the St. Lawrence and Great Lakes, and later down the Mississippi, eventually reaching the Gulf of Mexico. Since trapping and trading could be a year-round business, the trading

posts built by fur merchants were more like settlements than the fishermen's shore stations. In the early 1600s, in fact, the trading center known as Quebec could almost be called a town. Still, though the French were instrumental in establishing the European presence in North America—in the vast interior region they called Louisiana—they did not seriously regard the New World as a place to be settled, developed, lived in.

The British, more clearly than others, saw the New World as a possible annex to their homeland. Latecomers to America, they were especially successful in planting colonies. While British adventurers and traders left their country, it was settlers, people to whom the New World would be home, who were the mainstay of the colonies. The British had among them people whom they wanted to be rid of. Britain at the time was troubled by religious dissension and economic discontent. The establishment of the Church of England had troubled many Roman Catholics,

The Spanish gold-seekers were joined by the Portuguese, French, and Dutch, but gold was elusive. Some was found in Mexico and Peru, but in nothing like the quantity anticipated by the early European colonists. Then the Pilgrims arrived from England, and they found the gold mine they were looking for almost at once. The Pilgrims came to the New World for a different kind of wealth: for homes where they could practice their own religion, for land that they could till, for institutions that would insure their liberties. To the Pilgrims the gold mine of the New World was a new life.

who remained faithful to the Pope, and many Puritans and like-minded Protestants, who felt that the break from Catholicism had not been complete enough. The Crown met dissension with persecution, but dissension continued. The dissenters, then, were to be among the settlers of the New World.

Jamestown, the first successful English colony in North America, was established in Virginia in 1607, and it came close to collapsing within a year. After building Jamestown, the colonists attacked the soil with great energy, but they knew little about the methods that would work in the region, and their initial plantings yielded nothing. Illness, too, was a problem: malaria, a disease unknown in England, wiped out almost half of the original 104 settlers within six months. Although more ships brought more settlers, the fortunes of the Jamestown Colony did not im-

For the most part the Pilgrims lived austere lives: they believed in the virtues of hard work and prayer, and considered most forms of entertainment frivolous. Nevertheless, the challenge of building a new society ultimately modified the absolutism of the Pilgrims' beliefs. It took teamwork to create a livable environment in the American wilderness—teamwork to make laws, defend homes, raise barns. People working together learned to enjoy one another, and community activities —especially banqueting—inevitably became fun.

prove, and only martial law kept the colonists from abandoning the whole idea. The commercial success of Virginia's chief crop, tobacco, in Europe, and the gradual realization that settlers should move inland away from the swamps to avoid malaria eventually turned the tide for the Jamestown colonists, and after the first difficult generation Virginia began to prosper.

Plymouth Colony in Massachusetts was founded by the Pilgrims in 1620. Here, too, the early going was tough, but the industrious newcomers eventually overcame the obstacles and flourished. Following their example, other English Puritans anxious to flee the persecution at home sailed for America and established settlements in Connecticut, New Hampshire, and Maine (in colonial times a part of Massachusetts). Thus the part of the New World then and still known as New England was settled almost entirely by people alienated from the Anglican church. The dissidents who had formed New England were themselves confronted by disruptive individuals, led by Roger Williams. Forced from Massachusetts in 1636, Williams took to the wintry woods and found sanctuary in a region which came to be called Rhode Island.

England's persecuted Roman Catholics began to settle in the Maryland colony in the 1630s. These colonists were probably the most fortunate new arrivals in the colonies. For they learned immediately from their neighbors the Virginians how to plant corn and tobacco, and they learned, too, where *not* to settle.

Still another persecuted religious group, the Quakers, settled in Pennsylvania, founded in 1681 by William Penn. The three lower counties of Pennsylvania in later years were established as a separate colony called Delaware.

Dissatisfied with the Virginia farmland, a group of Virginia colonists traveled south and settled Carolina (not divided into north and south until 1691), which was given a royal charter as a colony in 1663.

The British along the eastern seaboard of North America had competition from the Dutch. In 1624 New Netherland was founded just south of New England. Although New Netherland's capital, New Amsterdam, on Manhattan Island, had a fine harbor, the Dutch could not take full advantage of it, for the small colony was not producing much to export. And when a British fleet arrived in the harbor in 1664, the Dutch surrendered the city before a shot was fired. The British took over New Netherland, renaming it New York.

Along the Delaware, a small group of Swedish settlers found a home. It was these colonists who built the log cabin, so practical that generations of later pioneers moving into the wilderness adopted it for their own.

The comparative fortunes of the English and Dutch colonies in North America revealed a great deal about the sort of society that was developing in the New World. Although many English settlers were fugitives from persecution, they enjoyed unusual freedom in America. Indeed, the Pilgrims had asserted themselves as free men shortly after their arrival by signing the Mayflower Compact. Before debarking, they agreed "to submit to such government and governors, as we should by common consent agree to make and choose." Persecuted though they might have been, these settlers were Englishmen, and Englishmen more than any other Europeans believed in the right of people to govern themselves lawfully—and possessed a tradition to support that belief.

The settlement of New Netherland favored the development of a colonial aristocracy. Every person who could bring fifty people to the colony was given a feudal estate on the Hudson; the estate was to be farmed by the settlers. Arbitrary and often harsh rule of a succession of appointed governors alienated settlers and

One of the methods employed by the Pilgrims for punishing youthful transgressions was dunking the offender in the well.

patroons alike. When the British fleet arrived and called for surrender, Governor Peter Stuyvesant's plea to his subjects fell on deaf ears: none were willing to resist.

The last of the thirteen colonies was Georgia. Established in 1733 by a group of British philanthropists, Georgia was not set up as a haven for fugitives from religious persecution, but for poor people, especially the debt-ridden, who wanted to make a new start in life.

The thirteen colonies thrived in the eighteenth century. As the population grew—from 250,000 in 1700 to ten times that by the time of the Revolution—as harvests grew more and more bountiful, as villages became towns and towns grew into small cities, the productivity of the colonists increased apace. The only

restrictions on the continued growth and prosperity of the people were imposed not by nature or by limitations in their energy, but by Great Britain; at least that was how many colonists felt. Understandably, the colonists found it increasingly frustrating to see the raw materials that they supplied being shipped off to England and returning as manufactured products that they had to purchase. As the century progressed, griping became a familiar feature of colonial American life.

More slowly than the English, the French thinly settled a vast region stretching from Quebec to the Mississippi Valley. Before long, French colonists drifting eastward and British colonists developing the western regions of the colonies became familiar sights to one another. Then the French constructed a chain of

To the Puritans, ignorance and sinfulness went hand-in-hand, and though the rigors of settling the wilderness demanded long hours of hard work from every member of the family, the colonists were conscientious about the education of their children. At first elementary education was provided at home. A higher education was available at Harvard College, established in Cambridge in 1636—a mere six years after the city of Boston was founded. Only eleven years later the General Court of the Massachusetts commonwealth enacted a law instituting a public education system. Thus, more than a century before the American Revolution, colonial America began to cultivate an educated citizenry, grounded in English legal and intellectual traditions, and aware of its rights. During the next 300 years, the right to a free education for all established itself as an American tradition.

"trading posts"—which really were fortresses—in a line north to south, from Quebec all the way to the lower Mississippi. These outposts essentially were barriers; their message to the British colonists was: this is as far as you may go; the British colonies end here. To make the message even clearer, the French moved armed soldiers into the outposts. The British colonists, proud of their progress and confident that there were no limits to their potential capabilities, did not appreciate the message. It was bad enough that their own monarch imposed restrictions on them; the last thing they needed was a restriction by a foreign king.

Fort-building was soon one of the major vocations of the French. In 1753 they began to construct a new series across the Ohio Valley from the Allegheny River to Lake Erie. The following year a detachment of Virginia militiamen with a young officer named George Washington second in command tried to stop construction in the valley, which the British Americans considered their own, but were driven back by the French. That battle—a personal setback from which Washington thought he might never recover—launched the struggle known in America as the French and Indian War.

At first the French, though outnumbered, won frequent and easy victories. Much more experienced frontiersmen than the British colonists, the French understood the kind of war that must be waged in a wilderness. Commanded by British generals, the British colonists were forced to form lines and follow the conventions of European warfare. Moreover, the French had always maintained much better relations with the Indians than had the British. The French fur trade, after all, had been dependent on cooperation with the Indians, who did most of the trapping. Indians, allied with the French, for a while were victorious over the British officers and their colonial soldiers. Learning from their adversaries, however, the British eventually gained the upper hand. By 1758 the war seemed to have turned into a stalemate, but the following year, in a carefully planned, finely executed campaign, the British attacked and seized a number of strategi-

The colonists and the natives of the North American continent regarded one another, at first, with a mixture of caution and curiosity. John Brereton, a member of one of the first expeditions to New England, wrote in 1602 that the Indians his party encountered on Cuttyhunk Island, southwest of Cape Cod, were "exceeding courteous, gentle of disposition, and well conditioned, . . . [and] pronounce our language with great facilitie. . . ." The Indians taught the newcomers a great deal about survival in the New World: the preparation of native fowl (in particular the wild turkey), the growth and uses of corn and tobacco, the navigation of streams and rivers. Not all of the European-Indian encounters were rewarding, however. Dutch attempts to establish settlements in the Delaware and Hudson valleys were particularly likely to provoke Indian resistance.

cally situated forts and broke the French communication lines. When the British captured Quebec, the French effort became hopeless. Quebec was the key to French America; without it the French could not maintain their control of the Great Lakes and the St. Lawrence River. Although the French-British war continued in Europe, where it was known as the Seven Years' War, the French withdrew their troops from North America in 1760.

The war was a disaster for France. Stronger than Great Britain at the time of its outbreak, France not only lost its prosperous American fur trade, but suffered further setbacks in the European phase. In 1762 France tried to reverse its decline by forming an alliance with Spain; in exchange for Spain's help, France had to yield the entire Louisiana Territory to Spain. The new alliance was not enough. The Treaty of Paris of 1763 ended the war; it also transferred Canada to the British.

The French and Indian War bolstered the pride of the already proud British Americans. The colonists felt that they had won the war and even began developing the newly won wilderness west to the Mississippi. London tried to put a stop to this westward movement, partly because it did not wish to lose control of its colonial subjects, and partly out of concern for the Indians, whose aid was needed in the fur trade. In 1763 a royal proclamation was issued which prohibited colonial settlement between the Appalachians and the Mississippi. The Americans were infuriated. Why, they asked, are we taking orders from a government an ocean away? America had its own resources, its own colleges, its own scientists and doctors and lawyers. Philadelphia was now larger than any British city except London. In a surge of pride, colonials looked to the day when the British Empire's capital would not be in London but in America.

A year after the proclamation that failed to prevent the Americans from settling westward, another proclamation came from London. Parliament—which did not permit colonials to be represented—decided that it was time for Americans to begin paying taxes.

THE MAKING OF A NATION

2.

THE MAKING OF A NATION

HE AMERICAN REVOLUTION WAS NOT WAGED to secure liberties. It was fought, rather, to preserve liberties already possessed—liberties which, the Americans believed, were being challenged by the mother country.

Almost from their start, the thirteen American colonies had been an unusual historical phenomenon. The idea of imperialism, of course, is age-old: empires came into being almost as soon as there were civilizations. Historically, colonies were foreign places populated by foreign peoples, ruled by representatives of the imperial power, or by appointed native leaders whose fidelity was pledged to the imperial power.

In contrast to historical precedent, and to the practice of other imperial nations of Europe, those Englishmen who settled in America and their descendants were to "enjoy all liberties, franchises, and immunities . . . to all intents and purposes, as if they had been abiding and born, within this our realm of England." Such an extraordinary status was granted because the settlers were in fact Englishmen; they were not a suppressed native population but an English population exported expressly to settle and develop the New World.

The English immigrants who landed in the New World confronted a vast wilderness, a great challenge, which most settlers accepted with great vigor. As the American historian Frederick Jackson Turner wrote, "The wilderness masters the colonist. . . . It strips off the garments of civilization and arrays him in the hunting shirt and the moccasin. . . . The fact is that here is a new product that is American."

Until—and even after—the French and Indian War, this "new product," this American, did not seriously entertain notions of freeing himself from the British Crown. Nor, for its part, did the Crown wish to curb the spirit or limit the freedom of the American. King and colonist alike were profiting from the association. Ironically, it was the shared British-American victory in the French and Indian War that created the first real problems.

Traditionally, the British had, for the most part, permitted the Americans to govern themselves. Following the same traditions, England assumed responsibility for the foreign affairs of the Empire. When the French were driven from North America in 1760 and American settlers began spilling into the lands between the Appalachians and the Mississippi, London saw this as a matter of foreign affairs; for the ownership of these lands had not yet been determined. The establishment of the "Proclamation Line" by Parliament in 1763 recognized that there were Indian inhabitants of the region, and also recognized Spanish ownership of Louisiana. But the colonists saw the proclamation as a violation of their right of self-government. Moreover, a series of Indian raids in 1763 compelled the British to return troops to America to defend the borders of the colonies. Finally, the cost of the Seven Years' War had seriously dented the British treasury; since the colonists had benefited so much from that war, Parlia-

ment felt that the colonists should help to pay for it—and for the subsequent defense of the colonies. Thus was enacted the Stamp Act of 1765, which introduced the first substantial duties and taxes on the colonists.

The colonists were furious: riots broke out, and in some colonies the Stamp Act was conspicuously ignored. Meanwhile, in London, disagreement over how the colonies should be treated led to turmoil in the government.

American defiance of the Stamp Act caused one government to fall; the government which replaced it repealed the Stamp Act; but soon a new set of duties and taxes were imposed. "Taxation without representation is tyranny!" cried the colonists, who continued to resist taxation. Tensions rose and tempers grew short: there were violent incidents between British soldiers and colonists in Boston in 1770 and Rhode Island in 1772. In the fall of 1773 a group of Bostonians climbed aboard a British ship and dumped 342 chests of tea into the harbor rather than pay the im-

In the third quarter of the eighteenth century, colonial resistance to English rule began to smolder, especially in Massachusetts and Virginia, two important centers of American colonial life. Although these two colonies were very different from each other, their grievances gradually linked them, and eventually united them with the other colonies. Partly because of its central location, Philadelphia became the unofficial "capital" of the collective colonies. There Massachusetts and Virginia delegates met with their discontented fellow colonies to discuss means of protest. The idea of preserving liberty did not originate in the City of Brotherly Love, but it came to be institutionalized there, and is commemorated by the bell that rang there, cracked there, but survived there.

port tax. A year later representatives from all the colonies except Georgia met in Philadelphia at the First Continental Congress. The Congress voted to cut off all trade with Great Britain until the colonies' grievances had been redressed. (Even at this late date the Americans did not want a complete break with the Crown; they merely wanted a guaranteed preservation of liberties and an American parliament.) The Americans stopped importing British goods, and in 1775 they stopped exporting.

In April of that year British troops advanced on Concord, Massachusetts, to confiscate the Americans' military stockpiles, and the first important battle in America's War of Independence began with, as Emerson put it, "the shot heard round the world." And *still* the Americans did not seek independence. In May the Second Continental Congress sent an "olive branch" message to George III saying, "We mean not to dissolve that union which has so long and so happily subsisted between us." With its armies apparently in control (though its losses in the early battles were substantial), England was not in the mood to grant concessions.

Defiance of the Crown in the 1770s was most blatant in Boston, where the Sons of Liberty met in Faneuil Hall to organize tax strikes and the Boston Tea Party. As the British became more inflexible, support for the Sons of Liberty grew. By the time the lantern in the Old North Church signaled the British military advance, and Paul Revere and William Dawes rode out to warn their neighbors, a significant number of Bostonians were ready to join the fight.

In the winter of 1775–76 Americans were reading a pamphlet by Thomas Paine, a gifted journalist recently arrived in America. In *Common Sense,* Paine argued that complete independence was the only guarantee of American liberty. During the first half of 1776 reluctant Americans supported the argument in ever-growing numbers. Paine's words, stark, unambiguous, were directed to the mass mind. Independence "rolled in like a torrent." In Philadelphia the Congress appointed a committee to prepare a proclamation. Thomas Jefferson of Virginia was its principal author.

"We hold these truths to be self-evident, that all men are created equal, that they are endowed by their Creator with certain unalienable Rights, that among these are Life, Liberty, and the Pursuit of Happiness."

With those words—so familiar to us now, but more revolu-

"The history of our Revolution," John Adams once wrote, "will be one continued lie from one end to the other. The essence of the whole will be that Dr. Franklin's electrical rod smote the earth and out sprang General Washington." In his own time Benjamin Franklin was the most celebrated of all Americans, and, as Adams's observation suggests, Americans thought that Franklin could do— and did—just about everything. The scientist-journalist-wit-inventor-statesman-philosopher of Philadelphia was so highly regarded that when he became a revolutionary, legions of previously uncertain Americans followed suit. Indeed, Franklin's reputation was not confined to his own country. In England a medallion was issued in his honor in the fourth year of the Revolution!

tionary than any ever written to state the existence of a nation—and with the words that followed them, the Continental Congress in Philadelphia declared, on July 4, 1776, that the United States of America, a free and independent nation, existed.

*   *   *

The British navy was the world's best; the British army was seasoned and strong; Great Britain could produce the paraphernalia of warfare as quickly as it was needed. But America was three thousand miles away from England, and the Americans, like the French before them, knew how to fight the warfare that was so efficient in the American wilderness. (In time, however, Americans fought as the Europeans did.) Held together by their commander in chief, George Washington, the Americans weathered their early defeats, regrouped, and began wearing down the British. When France sent help to the Americans in 1780 and 1781, and the British suffered several defeats, the British government toppled, and was replaced by a government which favored peace—and was resigned to American independence. The participants met in Paris, and the War of Independence was officially concluded on September 3, 1783.

At first the thirteen states operated as a nation under the Articles of Confederation, which had been drafted in 1777 and

After the Battle of Bunker Hill in June 1775, George III declared the American colonials to be "in open rebellion." Not so, replied the Continental Congress in its "olive branch" petition to the king; Americans were fighting to regain their rights as free Englishmen—rights which, they felt, the Crown had abridged. And even as American colonials took up arms and exchanged fire with British troops their aim was not independent nationhood; their flag was the English Union Jack against a field of stripes. But when the Crown made it clear that it would tolerate nothing less than complete colonial submission, there was no other choice but national independence. With all hope of reasonable conciliation gone, the colonial flag came down and the "Betsy Ross" flag, the Stars and Stripes, went up.

ratified in 1781. Designed more to protect the sovereignty of each state than to ensure an effective collective government, the Articles proved to be altogether unworkable as a unifying device. The shortcomings of the Articles soon become apparent. With each state a separate entity, the responsibility for resolving issues of a collective nature was uncertain. Perhaps most important, the central government under the Articles of Confederation had no power to deal with bickering between states—and there was no shortage of that. In 1787, six years after the ratification of the Articles, delegates from twelve states—Rhode Island stayed home —met again in Philadelphia, this time to draft a constitution that would really create a single nation out of the thirteen entities. By 1788 the eleven states that had ratified the Constitution were holding congressional elections. In January, 1789, George Washington was elected the first president of the United States. North

With the Declaration of Independence of July 4, 1776, the United States of America was born. After a baptism by fire that lasted until late in 1781, the new nation got down to the business of governing itself. The Articles of Confederation bound the states in a union too loose for the requirements of the country, and in 1787 the state delegations went back to Philadelphia to draw up a new constitution. Largely the work of James Madison of Virginia, the wording of the document was explicit yet flexible enough to gain the support of most of the delegates, whose ideologies varied. The new government, headed by President George Washington, took office in April 1789, in New York City.

Carolina ratified the Constitution later that year. Rhode Island remained outside, but finally agreed to ratify in 1790, when the other states said that if it did not, it would be treated as a foreign nation.

The government now had a "New Roof," and the sturdy structure was heralded as a masterpiece. Americans were sure that their society had lessons to teach the world, among which were: 1) A large country could be ruled by a Republican form of government without a monarchy or an aristocracy. 2) Religious worship needed no legal establishment. 3) Church and State could subsist without alliance. 4) People are happier and more contented under a "mild and equitable government," which is far stronger than arbitrary government and in less danger of being overturned. 5) Experience had proved "that to admit the Jews to all the privileges of natural-born subjects is far from being a dangerous experiment, as has been generally supposed."

Elhanan Winchester, the American writer who in 1792 listed these achievements, hoped the rest of the world would "learn and practise these lessons in a still more perfect manner than they are yet practised in America itself."

Getting from one place to another over the American terrain was tough, but transporting goods was even harder. Still, a growing nation needed to trade, and so ways had to be found. The Mississippi River and its many tributaries provided the first major network of trade routes linking regions, and flatboats were the first widely used transporters. Traffic was almost entirely downriver, however; rather than tow the empty flatboats back north, shippers sold the vessels for lumber at the southernmost port, and the crews returned home on horseback. The difficulties of merchant shipping were eased in 1811, when it became possible for cargo and passengers alike to sail every which way on the newfangled miracle, the steamboat.

The population of the United States was four million when Washington took office in New York. During Washington's two terms, Americans in significant numbers began drifting westward, mostly into Kentucky and Tennessee and then Ohio. By the end of the eighteenth century, the region west of the Appalachians to the Mississippi was becoming American. Beyond the Mississippi was the Louisiana Territory, which was returned to French control in 1800, when Napoleon negotiated a secret treaty with Spain. Many Americans were seriously alarmed at the prospect of a French presence on the continent again—especially since France was now ruled by Napoleon, who, it was widely assumed, had dreams of world conquest. By this time Thomas Jefferson was the American president, and he let the news go forth that the United States would not tolerate French occupation of the city of New Orleans, at the mouth of the Mississippi. But Napoleon was a powerful antagonist. His armies had not yet been beaten, and

In 1817, justifying American expansion into Indian territories, President James Monroe wrote that "The hunter or savage state requires a greater extent of territory to sustain it, than is compatible with the progress and just claims of civilized life . . . and must yield to it." In fact, the Americans who now ruled the continent had European traditions of land ownership completely foreign to Indian customs. As the Iroquois expressed it, the land was the mother of peoples, and a mother cannot be sold. Ultimately the notion of land as property prevailed; the great Indian nations dwindled and, in most cases, disappeared.

Napoleon himself was being hailed as the greatest military strategist since Julius Caesar. In 1803 Napoleon decided to send troops into Louisiana to solidify his grasp on a large piece of the New World, but first he had to reestablish French control of Haiti, which had revolted several years earlier. The French leader intended to quickly eliminate the rebels in Haiti and then move on to occupy Louisiana. But in Haiti the French got a taste of New World inhospitality: the guerrilla fighters of Haiti were not so easily dealt with, and yellow fever reduced the French numbers.

Napoleon decided that Old World conquest was challenging enough for the time being and abandoned his plans for North America. When Robert Livingston, the American minister in Paris, offered to buy New Orleans, he was astonished to receive a counterproposal: how much was the United States willing to pay for the entire Louisiana Territory? The answer was roughly fifteen million dollars, and on April 30, 1803, the territory owned by the United States was abruptly doubled.

Less than three months after the completion of the Louisiana Purchase, President Jefferson bid farewell to an expedition that he had organized to explore the vast lands west of the Mississippi and to chart a northwest passage to the Pacific. The mission was headed by Meriwether Lewis and William Clark, who were given explicit instructions by the president. Lewis and Clark were to assemble their men and supplies in St. Louis, and from there proceed westward, taking careful notes of the Indian tribes they encountered, recording plant and animal life, minerals, climate, geography, and anything else that would contribute to a complete portrait of the continent. They were also to search for a western river that might afford direct access to the Pacific through the wilderness. The search for such a river occupied much of the Lewis and Clark expedition's energies, and the energies of many later parties, but no such river was ever found. Another prize Jefferson eagerly desired was a North American mammoth—the giant elephant whose fossilized bones Jefferson had found in Kentucky. But the mammoth had been extinct for thousands of years. Notwithstanding the failure of their expedition to find the river and the animal, Lewis and Clark had a magnificent journey. They crossed the Great Plains, the Rockies, the incredibly dense forests of the Northwest; they met the Sioux and Mandan and Nez Percé and many other Indian peoples; they dined sumptuously on buffalo and river trout and cornmeal and berries; they discovered and crossed the Continental Divide; they found creeks and streams and rivers with water so clear that they could count the many species of fish as they swam by; they saw great moose and little weasels, yellow bears and wild hens; and at last, on November 8, 1805, they saw the Pacific.

The Lewis and Clark expedition returned to St. Louis on September 23, 1806. The report of its leaders to the president was thorough and evocative. National heroes, Lewis and Clark were now the inspirations for countless Americans who wanted to go where they had been, see what they had seen, settle in and develop the vast wilderness that now belonged to the American people.

* * *

Later—in the 1840s—the attitude of the American people toward expansion would be given a name: "manifest destiny." In fact this attitude, this belief in the right of the American nation to occupy the continent on which it was situated, began to take shape much earlier. But from early in the nineteenth century, the American frontier kept moving outward at a faster pace. Wherever Americans could ride a horse or haul a wagon Americans would go; wherever the soil was fertile and the horizon endless, Americans would settle. "Back of beyond" was the distant destination.

Americans were not, however, alone on the continent. In addition to the many Indian nations whose home America had been for thousands of years, Great Britain and Spain still claimed parts of the land, and to the south a new nation—as new and ambitious as the United States (though less wealthy)—was trying to establish itself. These other presences, so often ignored by American frontiersmen, could not be ignored by the American government.

Spain, which almost alone had possessed power in the New World in the sixteenth century, had seen its power steadily decline in the eighteenth century. In Paris in 1783, however, the decline had been temporarily halted when Florida had been returned to Spain. At that time Florida consisted of two parts: East Florida, approximately the peninsula land of the present state of Florida; and West Florida, a strip of land extending along the coast of the Gulf of Mexico to the Mississippi. Technically this "panhandle" strip blocked access to the gulf for the Americans settling the Mississippi Territory (now the states of Mississippi and Alabama), and it also presented a danger to American security since it terminated at the all-important city of New Orleans. Should any nation seize New Orleans, it could bottle up the Mississippi River, which had become the continent's principal corridor for North–South transportation. While the American government was concerned about these factors, American settlers apparently were not: they moved into the strip and settled it, and in sufficient numbers to make most of the West Florida popula-

Almost before there were roads to take them, the American people were on the move, making their way along broad, stump-filled, rocky paths. The surest means of transportation was the horse, but families of settlers and farmers anxious to market their harvests needed to transport more than could be stuffed into a saddlebag. Thus was developed the canvas-covered, homely, efficient Conestoga wagon, a primitive pickup truck and mobile home in one. The trip was bumpy, but the travelers were glad just to be moving: much of their time was spent lifting the vehicles from ruts and potholes or standing waist-high in mud, trying to prevent the heavy wooden wheels from sinking deeper. Indeed, until the government undertook a road-building program, the way west was paved mostly with the labor and patience of the settlers.

tion declare themselves loyal to the United States in 1809. A year later President James Madison encouraged the frontiersmen when he declared that West Florida had been acquired by the United States as part of the Louisiana Purchase. Thus supported, the settlers overpowered the weak Spanish forces and declared themselves annexed to the United States. A troop of American soldiers rode into West Florida to raise the Stars and Stripes over Baton Rouge, and the Spanish did not resist.

Pressure to annex East Florida thereafter gained momentum. But a more serious problem faced the United States: grow-

ing tension between the Americans and the British over freedom of the seas.

Engaged in a fierce war with Napoleon's France, the British had seen many of their impressed sailors desert to the United States. To counterbalance these desertions, British captains had been stopping American ships, ostensibly to search for deserters. Once on board a ship, however, the British would claim that virtually the entire American crew was comprised of deserters and would impress these sailors into the British navy. As tension increased, and war seemed inevitable, Americans who wanted to annex East Florida pointed out that when war did come, Great Britain might easily invade Florida, and from Florida the United States. The only way to avoid this, the annexation advocates said, was to make East Florida American. At first President Madison declined, still hoping that war could be averted. But events were moving against peace.

Not only events—human values, too. The struggle between the Americans and the Indians was always characterized by an essential difference in attitude that made the American advance almost inevitable. Americans, like their English ancestors, believed in the ownership of land. Most of the Indian tribes did not. Occasionally a tribe could be convinced to "sell" certain lands in exchange for goods or favors, but to many other tribes the very idea was an absurdity. As the great Shawnee chief Tecumseh put it, "Sell a country! Why not sell the air, the clouds, and the great sea . . ." Tecumseh traveled throughout the Midwest pleading with other Indian nations not to give up land. He was very successful, and for a time William Henry Harrison, governor of the Indiana Territory, could find no Indians to legitimatize American expansion. In 1809 Harrison managed to find a seller from the small Miami tribe. Tecumseh refused to acknowledge the sale, and formed an alliance with the British to defend the Indian homelands against American attack. In 1811 Harrison marched into the acquired territory and claimed it for the United States. The Indians resisted, and in 1813 Harrison and Tecumseh confronted each other in the Battle of Tippecanoe; the chief was killed, and Shawnee resistance crumbled. Because of Tecumseh's British alliance, many Americans claimed that the chief's resistance was actually an act of war by Great Britain. Americans cried, "On to Canada!" In the fever of the times, expansionists were envisioning the entire North American continent in the possession of the United States, and finally war came.

The War of 1812 ended in a stalemate, with not much changed. Canada remained British, and the East Florida problem was not resolved. In 1818 Gen. Andrew Jackson led his Tennessee militiamen into East Florida to put a stop to some Seminole Indian raids, and while he was there he decided to occupy Pensacola and other Spanish towns. Spain objected, and President James Monroe apologized and suggested that the United States and Spain open negotiations. Jackson's troops remained in Florida while the negotiations went on. The United States paid Spain five million dollars for East Florida and took possession in 1821. The same year, Mexico, which had been in revolt against Spain since 1810, declared its independence from Spain, and the Spanish empire in the New World continued its collapse.

Throughout the 1820s American settlers drifted into Texas, which belonged to Mexico. At first the Mexicans welcomed the Americans, and encouraged them to develop the huge, sparsely populated land, but so many Americans came that the Mexicans eventually began to worry. In 1834 the Mexican reformer-turned-dictator Gen. Antonio López de Santa Anna dissolved the Mexican Congress and abolished the Mexican state governments. When the Americans in Texas heard that Santa Anna intended to institute military rule in Texas and eventually drive them out, they began to organize resistance. In 1836, after the Texans and Mexicans had engaged in several battles, the Texans declared their independence, establishing the Republic of Texas. Even as the constitutional convention that created the new country was meeting, Mexican forces attacked San Antonio. The defenders of the city retreated to a mission known as the Alamo. Day after day the Mexicans attacked the Alamo, and suffered enormous losses. Eventually the Mexicans broke through into the mission, and all 182 defenders were killed. Among them were such national heroes as Jim Bowie and Davy Crockett. The slaughter of the defenders united the Texans as never before, and "Remember the Alamo!" became the rallying cry of the revolution. By the end of April, 1836—less than seven weeks after the Battle of the Alamo—the tide had turned, and with a couple of swift victories under Gen. Sam Houston, the Texans secured their independence. In the fall of the year Houston was elected the first president of the republic, and soon after Texas applied for admission to the United States.

But admission to the Union was not so simple. President Andrew Jackson was a friend of Sam Houston's and promptly awarded diplomatic recognition to the new republic, but he could not very well encourage Congress to admit Texas as a state without creating a host of problems. For one thing, Texas was a slave-holding territory, and in those touchy times any issue involving slavery was explosive in the United States. Another problem was that Mexico had not yet recognized the independence of Texas. Should Mexico decide to attack Texas to regain possession, then that was a matter between Mexico and Texas. But if the United States were to accept Texas and then Mexico attacked, that would constitute an invasion of the United States. Since many Americans felt that Mexico would be within its rights to try to get Texas back, Jackson knew that a war between the United States and Mexico would be divisive—if indeed Congress would agree to declare it at all.

Meanwhile Mexico did not attack. Texas encouraged more Americans to immigrate, offering 1,280 acres of land free to all families and 640 acres to any single man. These offers, combined with an economic depression in the United States in the late 1830s, swelled the Texas population. In 1835 there were 30,000 people there; ten years later the figure was 142,000. As the young republic prospered, some Texans began to feel that perhaps

Texas should remain a separate nation; many wanted to expand westward and become a partner with the United States and British Canada in possession of the North American continent. President Houston, who did not believe in such schemes, but who still could not get the United States to annex Texas, began to develop close relationships with Britain and France. This alarmed the Americans, who did not wish to see Texas bound through treaties of friendship, trade, and defense with the two superpowers of Europe. It particularly alarmed Andrew Jackson, a former president now, but still a most influential personality. "Old Hickory" in 1843 came out in favor of annexation. And annexation became a

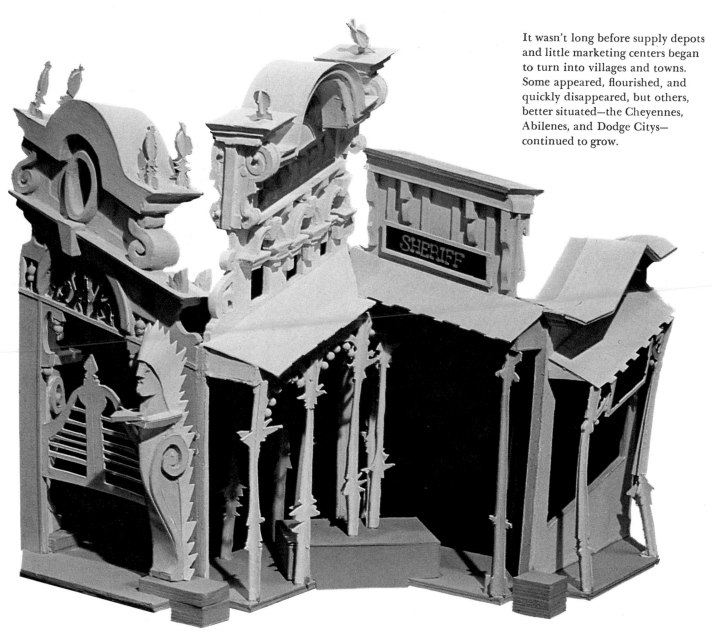

It wasn't long before supply depots and little marketing centers began to turn into villages and towns. Some appeared, flourished, and quickly disappeared, but others, better situated—the Cheyennes, Abilenes, and Dodge Citys—continued to grow.

The move westward was irresistible, and when gold was discovered in California in 1849, the traffic across the nation's primitive roads became heavier and heavier. To many visionaries, the gold mine of western expansion was to be found in commerce, and retail shops appeared wherever roads intersected, or the railroad train stopped.

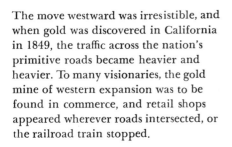

major issue in the election of 1844—one of the most important and exciting in American history, and one in which all the geographical issues that had been developing for years came together.

＊   ＊   ＊

"It is for the interest of mankind," wrote Walt Whitman, the young editor of the Brooklyn *Eagle*, that America's "power and territory should be extended—the farther the better." New York newspaperman John O'Sullivan agreed: our claims to the land, he wrote, sprang from "our manifest destiny to occupy and possess the whole of the Continent which Providence has given us."

"Manifest destiny": it was an irresistible idea; it cut across such issues as slavery and treaty-defined borders; it meant that the United States had the God-given right to the land it occupied and all adjacent land. As Andrew Jackson himself had said, Americans had been chosen to be "the guardians of freedom to preserve it for the benefit of the human race." Thus in the decades following the War of 1812 Americans had fanned out in all directions —not only into Florida and Texas, but all the way West. First the missionaries, explorers, trappers, and traders had gone the route of Lewis and Clark; then the pathfinders—the John C. Fremonts and Kit Carsons—had blazed new trails for settlers. By 1844 Americans had their roots down in California and Oregon, on the shores of the Pacific. That California belonged to Mexico, that Oregon (by virtue of an 1818 treaty) was America's and Great Britain's to share, didn't matter. Not to people who were "guardians of freedom," whose efforts, they said, were dedicated to all humanity.

The Texas controversy brought the whole issue of expansion to a head. Correctly reading the temper of the nation in the election of 1844, Polk, the Democratic presidential candidate, made expansion the major issue of the election campaign. "All of Oregon, All of Texas!" became a party slogan, and when the Whigs tried to counter with the suggestion that the slavery problem would be aggravated, the people were unconvinced. The slavery problem, after all, was an issue, a political thing; expansion was "manifest destiny." The election was close, but in the end Polk won. Three days before he took office, retiring President John Tyler signed the bill that annexed Texas to the United States. Mexico protested the annexation and broke diplomatic relations with the United States.

Polk tackled the Oregon problem first. Although, during the campaign, the Democrats had chanted "Fifty-four Forty or Fight!" Polk knew that the British would never give up all of the Oregon Territory. (The Oregon Territory was bounded on the north at 54°40′ N.—the approximate present border of Alaska.) Soon after he took office, he suggested that the huge region be divided at the 49th parallel, which represented the U.S.-Canadian border from the Great Lakes to the Rockies. The British refused; the best they would offer was the Columbia River as a border. By 1846, it was apparent to the British that American settlement—which, in its way, was tougher to deal with than military occupation—made the territory south of the 49th parallel truly American, and His Majesty's Government now proposed that parallel as satisfactory. Meanwhile, the most fervent American expansionists had resumed their cry for "All of Oregon!" and "Fifty-four Forty or Fight!" Indeed, there were those who now wanted to take *all* of Canada. Polk used his formidable legislative skill to overcome the opposition, however, and after a spirited

The rule of law was a sometime thing in some of the nation's younger and wilder Western towns, and it was hard, at times, to tell honest folk from the rogues. But the cities of the West were becoming important cogs in a new kind of national economy based on technology and commerce, and the colorful day of the gunfighter, gambler, and frontier sheriff was necessarily brief. By the end of the nineteenth century the West was for all intents and purposes tamed.

debate, Congress voted to approve the compromise boundary.

Next came California. So many Americans had settled in California that President Polk knew that their presence would create a crisis with Mexico. Hoping to avoid conflict, he sent a representative to Mexico City to offer the Mexicans forty million dollars for California and New Mexico (which included the present states of New Mexico and Arizona). The Mexican government would not even receive the representative. Many Americans —especially those in California—felt that the United States should simply annex the land, but Polk hoped to avoid that. In 1846, an incident in Texas provided the means by which America's continental expansion was soon to be completed. Between the Rio Grande and Nueces rivers in Texas was a small (by Texas standards) triangle of land whose ownership had been disputed. The Texans and Americans claimed that the Rio Grande was Texas's southern border; the Mexicans claimed that it was the Nueces. In April both the United States and Mexico sent troops into the region. Obviously, since each side claimed that that land belonged to it, each nation claimed to have been invaded. On May 13, Congress declared war. But "Mr. Polk's War" was not popular among opponents of slavery.

The war was quite limited for nine months. By September 14, 1847, American troops commanded by Gen. Winfield Scott, "Old Fuss and Feathers," had reached Mexico City, and the war was essentially won. On a big bay horse the plumed general rode into the city while tough marines took over the halls of the Montezumas. In the negotiations that followed, the Rio Grande became the final U.S.-Mexican border, New Mexico and California (but not the Baja California peninsula) became American, and in an unusual gesture for a country victorious in a war, the United States paid Mexico fifteen million dollars for the land it had taken —"conscience money" it was called.

Thus did the United States in 1848 extend its power and territory across the width of the North American continent—from sea to sea, and from the 49th parallel to the Rio Grande. Only seventy-two years after the thirteen colonies had declared their independence, the United States had fulfilled its "manifest destiny." Alaska would come nineteen years later, and Hawaii by the end of the century, but 1848 was the year the interconnected lands of the United States became whole.

And then, one year later, as if Providence indeed had been waiting, as though to ensure the solidification of the whole, the West Coast opened its arms to America east of it and beckoned with a glittering promise. Gold! America was alive with movement, the movement of wagons and horses and coaches west, west, west to riches and to new lives and to new unknowns.

The acquisition of territory created friction between the North and the South, and it sharpened the conflict between those opposed to slavery and the Southerners. There were, of course, other factors that helped to bring about the divided house. While historians still differ as to what brought about the Civil War, it is clear that slavery was one of its primary causes. In the 1850s, it was impossible to keep the issue out of the campaigns. The climax came with the election of Abraham Lincoln in 1860.

Lincoln bid goodbye to his neighbors in Springfield on February 11, 1861, setting off for Washington. On Inauguration Day, March 4, the new president stressed his duty to maintain the authority of the national government. To the South he appealed directly: "In your hands, my dissatisfied fellow-countrymen, and not in mine, is the momentous issue of Civil War." To the hushed audience, he spoke of reconciliation: "We are not enemies but friends."

"The mystic chords of memory stretching from every battle field and patriot grave to every living heart and hearthstone all over this broad land, will yet swell the chorus of the Union, when again touched, as surely they will be by the better angels of our nature." But his words fell on deaf ears. For more than four years war raged between the North and the South, now organized into a confederacy. To Southerners the war was brought on by Northern invasion of their land. To counter the North, the South had

In May 1869, the newly laid tracks of the Central Pacific and Union Pacific railroads were joined by a golden spike at Promontory Point, Utah, and, suddenly, the two distant coasts of a nation not yet one hundred years old were bound together. The railroad did much more than provide the country with geographical unity. It transformed the continent, bringing farmers to the Midwest and West to turn the Great Plains into the greatest food-supplier in all history, and transporting the farmers' grain to ocean ports, from which it was shipped all over the world. It transported the ranchers' cattle quickly from the Southwest to the stockyards of Kansas City and Chicago—and it ended, too, the ranchers' Indianlike concept of land as "open range," owned by no one and by all.

distinguished military leadership, especially Robert E. Lee and "Stonewall" Jackson. The North fumbled for some time until General Grant and General Sherman took charge. Behind the battle lines it was Lincoln who lifted the spirit of tired Northerners, holding aloft the ideal of Union, which triumphed in the end.

The triumph was costly. Over 359,000 Northern and 250,000 Southern lives were lost; the future of a whole generation in the South was impoverished. The North's hard-won victory gave Americans a legacy of union and freedom. Transcending national boundaries, it gave to the world the glory of Abraham Lincoln.

Hallowed names and places have become part of the Civil War heritage. Gettysburg, where in the summer of 1863 Southern gallantry met Northern stubborn defense, was made the site of a new national cemetery the same year. Lincoln dedicated it with the immortal words: "From these honored dead we take increased devotion to that cause for which they gave the last full measure of devotion—that we here highly resolve that these dead shall not have died in vain—that this nation under God shall have a new birth of freedom—and that government of the people, by

The railroad brought shrewd businessmen into the continent's interior to build banks and commercial enterprises to service and help construct an economy that was much more complex than many people imagined. It brought salesmen with calico and barbed wire; it brought women to wear the calico and men to clip the barbed wire; and it brought more guns to settle barbed-wire disputes.

the people, and for the people, shall not perish from the earth."

*   *   *

The acquisition of territory alone did not make the United States a whole nation, for if the lands between the oceans were a lure, they also presented obstacles to movement. There were fast-flowing rivers, huge mountains, sprawling prairies, endless deserts, deep canyons—all offering resources that could and would make a nation rich, yet all standing, challenging, serving as barriers first and only then as servants.

To westward-bound settlers, trails were one-way routes to new lives. To the developing nation, however, trails were not enough. Eventually the trails would have to be expanded and incorporated into a network of highways, railroads, and canals to serve not a nation of homesteads, but a nation of cities and commerce. Thanks to America's first great feat of engineering, the Erie Canal, barges transported freight back and forth between the Great Lakes and the Hudson River, thence to the Atlantic. The United States would prosper as a nation not merely because its crops were good, but because those crops could be transported quickly and efficiently. America would become great not only because its mountains yielded rich minerals but also because ores from the mountains could be efficiently turned into alloys and the alloys into man-made goods and machine-made wares. The country would be well-fed not simply because ranchers bred fine, fat cattle, but because the network of inland routes made it possible to transport whole herds to slaughter, and fresh meat to market. Drawn by the promise of the land, people moved west and laid the groundwork for an urban-industrial society, a society of Pittsburghs, Chicagos, and Kansas Citys.

The settlers of the West, then, settled down to raise crops and mine ores that were transported back east on steel wheels, and through carefully engineered locks. Imposing locomotives pulled goods from Wheeling on the Ohio River to Baltimore on Chesapeake Bay and back again. Paddle-wheel steamboats hauled cargoes up and down the Mississippi.

Even with all the advances in transportation—the locomotive was of course the main one—the natural obstacles were not easily conquered. A locomotive pulled a train from an Eastern city to the Ohio or Delaware or Mississippi and found—the Ohio or Delaware or Mississippi. And the big train sat and waited until its cargo was ferried across. Finally, another train took off, confronting the giant mountain barriers between prairie and the markets of San Francisco and the port of Seattle. So the rivers had to be bridged and tunnels had to be cut through mountains, and these bridges and tunnels had to be bigger, longer, and stronger than others built or dug before. Amazingly, it was done. The picturesque covered wooden bridges of America gave way to the iron-truss bridges; fifteen years after the United States spanned the continent, an iron bridge spanned the Ohio River; a decade after that the great Mississippi itself was bridged by James Eads; ten years after that came the wonder of the ages, the Brooklyn Bridge. Meanwhile, men such as the legendary John Henry and their natural rival, the compressed-air drill, were cutting holes through rock: when the Hoosac Tunnel, five miles long, was completed in Massachusetts in 1873, the word was out that anything could be cut through.

Before the engineers worked their marvels, the flying hoofs of the Pony Express linked St. Joseph, Missouri, to the Pacific coast. Samuel F. B. Morse's telegraph speeded messages across the country. And the Atlantic cable diminished the distance between Europe and America.

The engineering conquest of America was in many ways the greatest factor in the welding of a single nation from the many diverse geographical areas between the oceans. On May 10, 1869, the tracks of the Union Pacific Railroad were joined by a golden spike to the tracks of the Central Pacific Railroad at Promontory Point, Utah. The continent could be crossed in one week by train. The nation was not only whole; it was one. The American people—well, they were one, too. Like the country's motto, *e pluribus unum,* the people were one out of many. Very many.

FOLDOUT PAGE

THE MAKING OF A PEOPLE

3.
THE MAKING OF
A PEOPLE

POLITICALLY THE AMERICAN NATION came into being in the year 1776. Geographically it developed in stages. The first area of settlement was the Atlantic seaboard, from the rocky coast of Maine to the sandy beaches of Georgia. Although the original thirteen states claimed—sometimes in conflict with one another—land ownership all the way to the Mississippi, the wilderness for all intents and purposes started at the Appalachians. Even as the Louisiana Purchase was being negotiated, even as Lewis and Clark explored the continent westward to the Pacific, that formerly disputed land between the Appalachians and the Mississippi was being settled, and by 1821 had become the states of Illinois, Indiana, Ohio, Kentucky, Tennessee, Mississippi, and Alabama, and the Michigan Territory. The events of the 1840s completed the cross-continental evolution of the nation.

The national evolution of the American people was also accomplished in stages. (Indeed, it is still an ongoing process.) The American, that "new product," had existed well before American independence; yet the twentieth-century American is likely to be a very different product from his eighteenth-century forebear. But is the modern American any more or less an American? The answer, of course, is no, and to support it we need only compare the evolution of the American citizen with the evolution of the American geographical nation.

The United States was born as a seacoast nation; then it expanded to include the old, rolling Appalachians and the Mississippi Valley; then it took in the Great Plains and the Rocky Mountains with their snowy peaks and incredibly colored canyons, and then the Pacific coastline. At each stage it multiplied its acreage many times; at each stage it changed its physical complexion, almost always radically. But at each stage it remained the United States of America—the same United States of America that had declared itself a nation in 1776. The same is true of the American. He was probably of English, Scottish, or German ancestry if he fought in the Revolution, but he might well have been Dutch or French, or very possibly a mixture. (And one of the very first Americans killed in the struggle preceding the War of Independence was Crispus Attucks, a black man.) During the years of westward expansion the American of Scotch-Irish, German, English, French, or Dutch descent continued to prevail, al-

Thomas Jefferson had envisioned an America that would be an agrarian society—a society dominated by farm families producing enough food for their own needs, and a little extra for the marketplace. By the second half of the nineteenth century, a complex agrarian economy had indeed developed in the nation, but it was nothing like Jefferson's vision. The railroads and the Homestead Act had opened the American interior to virtually anyone who wanted to settle and farm, but fast access to ports, and from ports to world markets, had made American agriculture a great commercial venture in which output—not family self-sufficiency—was of prime importance. A further catalyst to the development of large-scale farming was the technology of farm machinery, growing by leaps and bounds.

though the increasingly frequent encounters with the Indian peoples of the continent had its effect on the evolution of an American character. Southwestern expansion, moreover, added a Spanish flavor to the process, for though the Spaniards had departed, they had left some of their genes behind—and many of their habits and traditions.

Then, about 1830, just as the geographical whole was taking shape, waves of immigrants began to arrive in the United States. The Irish came, and the Germans and Scandinavians, and then the eastern and southern Europeans, and—on the West Coast— Chinese and Japanese. The Civil War's outcome made American citizens of the unwilling immigrants from Africa, and like the European and Asian arrivals, the more firmly America-rooted Afro-Americans retained some of the culture they had brought with them, and gave some of those cultural elements to the evolving American. Like the nation itself, the American people changed their composition many times, often radically, while always remaining the American people.

A people, traditionally, is a collective bound by the land on which they live, the language they speak, the customs they honor, and the government to whose laws they are subject. Throughout history most peoples have been united more or less by chance, over many generations; their evolution has been almost organic. The American people were not the only exception to this general rule of history, but they were the most radical exception. The main reason that they were an exception was America itself—the idea of it, and, most important, the promise it made to uprooted newcomers. The United States was not populated by nomads who just happened into it (excepting, of course, its very first inhabitants, the Indians); it virtually recruited a citizenry by offering what no great nation in history had offered: freedom, the opportunity to rise as high as talent and enterprise and intelligence and drive could take you, and a Bill of Rights that ensured all comers their "unalienable Rights"—rights that no arbitrary judicial ruling, no word from a monarch's mouth, no legislature could take away. These rights were offered at a time when many of the world's people were being denied them. Along with the rights came jobs and land, at a time when political and natural disasters were making work elsewhere hard to come by, and when the land in many countries was suddenly withholding the harvests it had yielded for generations, even centuries. Call it luck or fate—the fact is that at the very moment when the American nation overspread and occupied the width of this continent, at the very moment when a network of arteries began to crisscross the new nation, at the very moment when the industrial age was beginning to fashion a new kind of economy in a new, underpopulated world, a series of disasters befell the Old World. It is easy, now, to look back wryly at the "manifest destiny" attitude of the 1840s; and yet, in the large view, it seems incredible that just as America needed to be peopled, the rest of the world became inhospitable. America needed people, in other words, precisely when people needed America. The compatible needs created the American people. In the largest view "manifest destiny" seems a fitting description for the remarkable and fast development of the American people.

*   *   *

During most of the nineteenth century, the United States was primarily a nation that exported raw materials and imported manufactured goods. As the century progressed, and America built more and more factories, the imbalance was slightly corrected, but this only exacerbated the economic problems of the shippers. After 1815 (the year the Napoleonic Wars ended in Europe), the United States became, for the first time, a truly significant trans-Atlantic trader. Freighters from eastern ports sailed regularly for Europe with their holds filled to overflowing with American exports: lumber, cotton, tobacco. As much of these raw materials as the Americans could load, the Europeans would buy. When the freighters returned to the United States, they carried the products made from American materials: furniture, fabric, cigars. Other cargoes also helped fill the freighters' holds. Before 1808, many ships' captains filled the empty holds with slaves, but the slave trade was outlawed that year, leaving the merchant vessels with insufficient cargoes. Enterprising ship-owners began to encourage immigration. They offered European peasants trans-Atlantic crossing at a low fee, provided the passengers were willing to bring their own food, demand nothing of the ship's crew, and remain in the hold. Immigrants were much better than ballast: immigrants loaded and unloaded themselves, and since, without them, the holds would be empty, whatever they paid was gravy. As the century progressed, and the United States began manufacturing more and more of its own goods, the empty-holds problem got worse, and more shippers began to take on more immigrants.

The first European country to send a sizable number of its citizens to the United States in the nineteenth century was Ireland—conveniently located for the shippers, since much U.S. raw material went to England. Ireland's problems seemed unending early in the nineteenth century, and things did not improve as decades passed. The main problem was population: the Emerald Isle was small; by 1800 it may have become the most densely crowded nation in all Europe. The land was subdivided into tiny farms that could barely feed the existing population, and it became apparent to young men that they would not be inheriting fine farmland on which to raise their families, but, rather, tired—and perhaps further subdivided—farmland. To make matters worse, Ireland had all but run out of timber. An exploding population; tiny, tired farms; no wood to make barrels to store the surplus when there was a surplus or to ship the harvest to market; no wood to build more homes. In the 1820s many Irish began dealing with these problems by sailing their own small boats across the North Atlantic to Canada to get wood. Some of the young men saw that Canada and especially the United States were labor-poor; some remained—intending, at first, to stay just a season or two—to work in the forests, mills, or shipyards; others returned home and spread the news to ambitious young men that there was plenty of work to be had across the sea. In the early part of the decade the great Erie Canal construction project was under way, offering thousands of jobs to all comers. It was back-breaking work, and paid only fifty cents to a dollar a day, but to the depressed Irish it was tempting. When the project was completed in 1825, and the Erie Canal proved so successful, canals

were begun throughout the East. The Irish were first on the job: twenty thousand Irishmen emigrated to America in 1827; in 1832 the number had jumped to sixty-five thousand. The merchant shipper's empty-holds problem was solved, and Ireland's population and unemployment problems were, if not solved, at least helped.

Then came the potato famine. The potato—*patata,* the conquistadores had called it—was an American crop, first transplanted to Europe in the sixteenth century by Spanish explorers. Within a hundred years the potato had become as important to the poorer nations of Europe as rice was to the Chinese; it was the basic staple of the Irish and German diet. In 1829 a mysterious "potato disease" struck part of the German crop; thereafter some other part of the crop was infected each year. North America itself got a taste of the blight in 1844, and a year after that it hit all Europe. In all these cases the fungus attacked only some of the crop—enough to constitute a disaster in Ireland—but still not all of it. In 1846, however, virtually the whole crop failed. Since the famine of the previous year had prevented the storage of reserves, the result was as horrible as anything seen in Europe since the

People who thought that the railroads were transforming America, overnight, into a highly developed, easily-traveled land had only to hop off the train and head for a town just a few miles off the main lines. The stagecoach that carried bundles, mail, and passengers from railroad depots to the nation's many growing villages, camps, and towns looked fancy; but it was only slightly more comfortable than the Conestoga wagon—and road-building technology hadn't come very far, either.

89

bubonic plagues of the Middle Ages. People starved to death by the thousands. A form of typhus, worsened by untended corpses, spread throughout Ireland, infecting those not starving. Now the rush to the ports was greater than the merchant ships could accommodate. Even so, in the years between the blight and the Civil War, some two and a half million Irishmen emigrated to the United States.

The Irish had had such misery at home that they were glad to do any work that paid a day's wage. Many stayed in the port cities where they arrived—Boston and New York in particular—and found work as laborers; the women often took on domestic work. There were Irish firemen and Irish streetpavers and—yes, of course—Irish police officers. Those who traveled west from the cities became coal miners, construction workers on the railroads, farmhands, builders of textile mills. The Irish tended to work harder for less pay than many American laborers. From their slim earnings, immigrants, especially the Irish women, sent passage money back home for other members of their families, left behind in blighted Ireland. Other American workers resented the Irish for their "job stealing," and they were actively discriminated against in the United States. "No Irish Need Apply" was a familiar closing to certain job or apartment advertisements throughout the earlier years of the nineteenth century.

Nevertheless, the Irish were quick learners and in time became "real" Americans—which means simply that they came to understand their rights, to stand up for them, and to help others achieve their rights, too. The Irish in America were particularly talented in political and labor organization. Although they never abandoned their nostalgic affection for the old country, the Irish made sure that all of their transplanted countrymen applied for American citizenship; in many eastern cities they soon formed important voting blocks, and in New York and Boston, for much of the nineteenth century and the early years of the twentieth, they dominated the city governments, first as civil servants, then as elected officials. The Irish political contribution probably reached its zenith in the year 1960, when an American of Irish ancestry, John Fitzgerald Kennedy, was elected president of the United States.

The large-scale German migration to the United States started at about the same time as the Irish, increased as famine hit the German potato crop, and also continued throughout the nineteenth century. Germany—which was not a nation until the

As villages became towns and towns became bustling cities, America became a more worldly place. By the end of the nineteenth century, international trade expositions were being held in American metropolises, and the United States began to realize that it was the main showplace for the dawning age of technology. The gazebo was a feature of the St. Louis World's Fair of 1904.

1870s—was not only overpopulated early in the nineteenth century, but its economy and politics were volatile. Periods of liberal reform were followed by periods of repression and religious intolerance. The unpredictability of the political climate drove many Germans to America. Catholic-Protestant conflicts drove more across the Atlantic in the thirties and forties. Cheap land in America's Middle West was a lure German farmers found hard to resist. And then of course there was the famine.

Most of the German immigrants—particularly in the period prior to the Civil War—were not political or religious refugees. Most were farmers, skilled craftsmen, or tradesmen. Starting in the early years of the nineteenth century, American trade with Germany became significant. American cotton was bought up as fast as it could be shipped and was turned into German fabrics.

American tobacco found a better market in Germany than anywhere else; the Germans not only made more cigars for export than anyone else, they also smoked the most themselves. German businessmen realized the value of sending representatives to live in the United States, in order to do business with suppliers at the source. When the representatives wrote to relatives, word got around that Americans were hungering for manufactured goods —not only major, factory-made goods, but small, everyday items: ready-made clothing, tools, leather goods, utensils. Many German businessmen were Jews, whose place in German society could be fully accepted today, denied tomorrow. Unlike most of the Irish emigrants of the 1840s and fifties, many Germans were not poor; often they were educated men with a little money in the bank and the means to start a business in the New World.

When the famine drove many rural Germans to America, the newcomers demonstrated another difference between themselves and the Irish. Whereas the Irish tended to come individually, then send for their relatives, the Germans regarded the idea of leaving their homeland for a new one without taking their families as almost incomprehensible. Because they traveled in family groups, they tended to stick together in America, to move as a group from port to destination. Though many stayed in eastern cities, German farmers liked the woodsy, lake-filled interior of the mid-north United States, for it reminded them of home; and they settled primarily in Wisconsin and Michigan. They were helped enormously by the Homestead Act of 1862—which provided that any citizen or alien intending to become a citizen was entitled to 160 acres of land in certain territories for a negligible fee; he could take automatic possession by living on it for five years. In the interior areas that they selected, the Germans set up "little Germanys"—communities that stretched for miles, populated entirely by Germans who continued to speak German and to duplicate as closely as possible the sort of life they'd had in Europe. New York City, too, had its "Klein Deutschland."

The German immigrants made considerable contributions

The Industrial Revolution found optimum conditions for development in the United States. Railroads, though important, were not the only factor: in America there were not so many old factories, tooled for old manufacturing methods, as there were in Europe, and new factories could be constructed from the ground up.

to the development of the American people. Although the farm Germans were inclined to keep to themselves, the city Germans founded music societies—such as the Germania Orchestra in New York, which became the New York Philharmonic—built breweries in New York and Milwaukee, and were instrumental in improving public educational facilities. Actually the German contribution was probably greater than is apparent, but the fact that Germany was America's enemy in two twentieth-century wars compelled the German-Americans to disband many of their ethnic organizations, to change their names, and generally to minimize their origins.

The influence of the German Jews, however, remains apparent. Probably no immigrant group was more successful in the United States—at least in terms of economic and business achievement—than this persecuted minority from Europe. Many started as peddlers, following the westward migration on the American continent, selling the settlers, cowboys and miners their boots and blue jeans; others turned their backpacks filled with merchandise into department stores; some went into banking.

The Scandinavians who emigrated to the United States re-

Like the factories built to serve a new urban-industrial society, America's cities could be built almost from scratch. And the American people, who had long assumed they were agrarian, took to city living with apparent ease.

sponded to advertising. The romance of the land—that is, of owning and farming a homestead—has appealed to people everywhere for centuries. But in nineteenth-century Scandinavia, land ownership was out of reach of most people. Traditional practices had persisted in every country; the only citizen with real influence was the landowner; and medieval-style guilds prevented young craftsmen from prospering. Merchant shippers began circulating news of America in Scandinavia in the 1820s and 1830s, news of land at $1.25 an acre, news of jobs galore for all skilled craftsmen. In the second half of the century, the trickle of emigrants that had made the trip in the first half became a stream, as economic hardship hit. Although they were scarcely happy with conditions at home, young Scandinavians had at least been able to survive by working in the lumber-related trades. But after 1850 iron began to replace wood in the construction of ships and buildings, and the Scandinavian wood industry began to decline. Now was the time for ambitious Scandinavians to try America. At the same time, Scandinavian Mormons escaped persecution at home by leaving for America. Scandinavian farmers settled in Minnesota, the Dakotas, and other northern regions.

Scandinavian immigrants carried to America skills learned

in the Old World. They were excellent farmers, the Danes excelling in dairying. As did other immigrant groups, they sought to Americanize. The Scandinavians anglicized their names, gradually stopped speaking their native tongues and replaced them with English, and formed or joined institutions that were conspicuously American.

The Scandinavian migration to the United States had a notable impact on the culture of the United States, and on the countries of Scandinavia. Late in the nineteenth century, these counries began to notice that too many of the young Scandinavians had gone across the sea. The loss of youth is handwriting on the wall: what, after all, can the future hold for a nation that has no talented youth? Around 1880 people in the various governments began to preach reform. In fact, a concerted effort was made to encourage Scandinavian emigrants to return home and "Americanize" Scandinavian society. Over the years thousands did return. Furthermore, the governments sent representatives to study American industry, which was viewed as responsible for the growing prosperity and rising living standard of the Americans in the last quarter of the century. Among the results of Scandinavia's America-studies were universal suffrage, agrarian reforms, tax reform, free universal education, religious tolerance. Did it work? Less than a century later, the American government was sending representatives abroad to study Scandinavia's social institutions!

*   *   *

After the Civil War, American industry began to prosper and to dominate the American economy. Before the war, the United States had stretched from the Atlantic to the Pacific and from the Great Lakes to the Rio Grande. In 1867 the territory of Alaska was added to the U.S. Before the end of the century, Hawaii and Samoa became part of a growing American empire.

Nearer home, the imperial dream of America fixed on the Caribbean, especially Cuba, "the Pearl of the Antilles." Cubans had been in revolt against Spain for years. Sympathetic Americans,

FOLDOUT PAGE →

inflamed by newspaper stories of atrocities committed by Spanish soldiers, wanted to intervene in the struggle. Americans had a large stake in Cuba's sugar industry, which was endangered by the conflict. Then, too, American naval strategists were anxious to add the island to the United States. On February 15, 1898, the U.S. warship *Maine* blew up in Havana's harbor, and 250 men were lost. Though who or what caused the explosion remained unknown, Americans immediately fixed on Spain as the culprit. "Remember the Maine! To Hell with Spain!" became a popular slogan. Spain was conciliatory as the war fever mounted in the U.S. The president, William McKinley, also preferred a peaceful solution, but the pressure from "war hawks" was too strong, and on April 25, 1898, the United States declared war on Spain.

Apart from the Navy, the United States was ill-prepared for war, but Spain's preparation was even more feeble. In some ten weeks, the war was over. Far across the Pacific, in the Philippines, Commodore Dewey destroyed the Spanish ships in Manila Bay. American deaths, some five thousand, came less from the battlefield than from disease.

The fruits of victory made Cuba for some thirty years a virtual protectorate of the United States.

The island of Puerto Rico, another Spanish possession, was annexed. So too were the Philippine islands—in exchange for $20 million. "The whole policy of annexation," Senator Henry Cabot Lodge wrote to his friend Theodore Roosevelt, "is growing rapidly under the irresistible pressure of events."

There were other benefits of the war besides additions of territory. In an earlier conflict, the War of 1812, Francis Scott Key saw "the bombs bursting in air" and wrote the words of our national anthem. Soldiers in the Spanish-American war marched off to John Philip Sousa's "Stars and Stripes Forever." Songs like "There'll be a Hot Time in the Old Town Tonight" were long remembered. Commodore Dewey became an admiral, and Theodore (Teddy) Roosevelt, leader of the Rough Riders, became a hero of Americans, who soon sent him to the White House.

The nation's industrial growth required the expansion of the railroads, and also the enlargement of mining and factory facilities, and required, too, the construction of fast-growing, efficient cities. There was plenty of work to be done, and workers were needed. Through America's "golden door" for almost fifty years the "wretched refuse" from Europe flooded in. Russians, Ukrainians, Poles, Hungarians, Slavs, Serbs, Rumanians, Armenians, Italians, Greeks—sixteen million of them came, many in "steerage" of a steamship, sharing the crossing with cattle; they came in funny-looking clothing, speaking languages sounding far stranger than any Americans were used to, sticking together protectively, full of hope and fear, both justified. Americans didn't like their coming too much, and the immigrants, for their part, didn't like each other very much, but in the end their coming worked out for America, because America needed hands.

Their sheer numbers made these new Americans unique among immigrant groups, but there were other differences, too. For one thing, many of these new arrivals were "alien" in almost every conceivable way. Most of their predecessors had been Western European Christians—that is, Roman Catholic or members of the various Protestant sects. Among the migrants of the later European transplantation, a substantial number were Balkan and practitioners of the Eastern Orthodox brand of Christianity, whose rituals and beliefs seemed dark and mystical to Western eyes. Others were Jews, whose practices appeared stranger still. For another thing, the majority of the newcomers had been outsiders even in their former homes. Bulgaria, Rumania, Serbia, and Greece had for several centuries been Christian islands in the Ottoman Empire of Islam. The Jews, unwelcome residents of the Eastern European nations and Russia, had had a fifteen-hundred-year history of persecution and expulsion within the Moslem and Christian worlds. Generation after generation, century after century of rootlessness, or of being colonial subjects in the lands of their ancestral roots, had affected the social attitude and lifestyle of the new immigrants. The habit of huddling together, of seeking security in numbers and unity was not easily broken. The fact that these newcomers looked and acted so strange—at least to American eyes—further emphasized their isolation. Since America was fast becoming an urban nation, and since the newcomers were almost uniformly poor, they settled together in the slums of the cities. As quickly as boats docked, inner-city pockets formed and enlarged. The Irish and Germans had already formed their "neighborhoods" in most cities; now Greek streets and Syrian blocks and Jewish sections and Hungarian avenues took shape—adjacent to Chinatowns and Little Italys—and made American cities international centers, latter-day Constantinoples where business was done in dozens of tongues, where the air smelled of curry and of oregano-spiced tomatoes and of boiling fish and of a hundred other exotic simmerings, where the costumes of a dozen cultures became the players' garb on a world stage compressed into a square mile or two. America—especially urban America—became a nation of strangers, the American people a strange conglomeration of peoples with seemingly nothing in common—nothing except America.

But America was enough, more than enough. What was most astonishing about this astonishing mixture was that its parts —for all their separateness, for all their insularity—did in fact mix. Life was difficult, American society a puzzle, but the unwanted of the Old World found here what they had come looking for: opportunity. If the odds were against the immigrants, if the struggle to survive left little energy for seeking the fruits of liberty, the men and women who endured the trials of the long journey and the tribulations of life at their destination nevertheless embraced the New World and its stated values. In America, said a grateful Hungarian, "I am mister too." America was a blessing because it would provide the opportunity for their children to become Americans; the reward for their struggle would be their children's not having to struggle. In their homes they spoke Greek or Polish or Yiddish, and they may have learned only enough English to pass the naturalization test, but they made sure their chil-

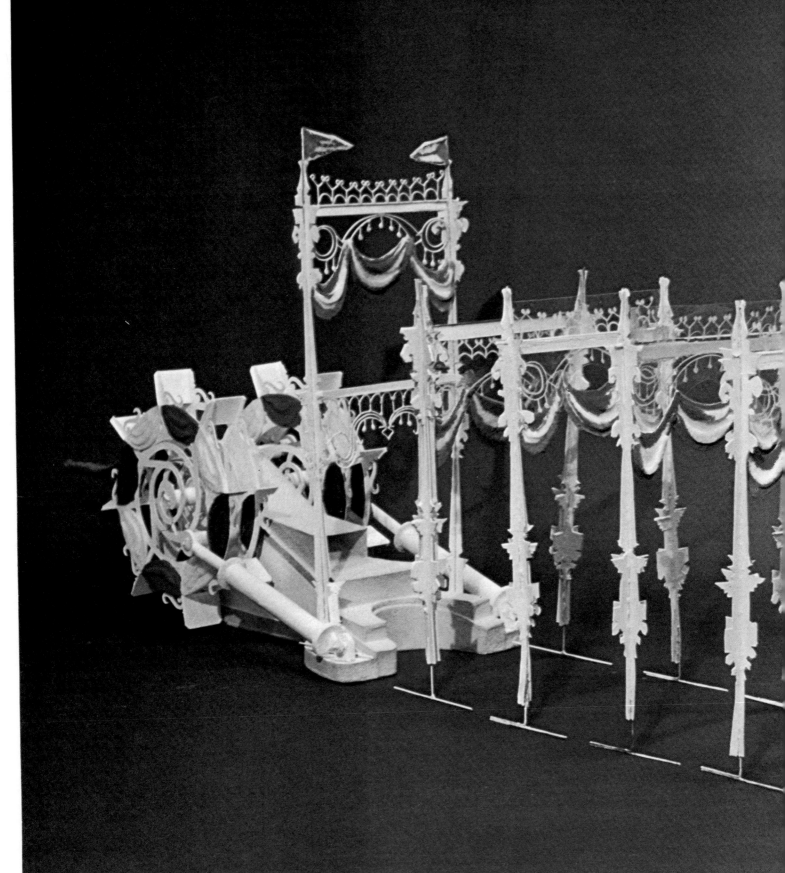

The newcomers who arrived in the United States throughout the nineteenth century brought with them ancient artistic traditions of drama, circus, minstrelsy, and dance; elements of each were combined under the big umbrella known simply as "the show business." The form in which varied acts were presented to the public was the vaudeville show, and the first means for taking the show to the greatest possible public was the showboat. Vaudeville became a highly polished form of entertainment on these colorful vessels, which sailed up and down the Mississippi; then, as rails crossed the nation, players piled scenery and costumes onto trains for one-night stands in towns scattered across the country, and show business became big business.

dren spoke English and understood what it was to be American—
to be a free man or woman with unlimited opportunity.

And America profited from their being here. For centuries,
Europe's Jews, forced into ghettoes, self-insulated for mutual pro-
tection, had cultivated a tradition of scholarship. This tradition
was the Jews' gift to America. As the Irish had by the strength of
their abilities transformed Eastern-urban politics, the Jews sent
their first generation native-born sons and daughters into American schools, and in no time at all (on history's clock) traditional
Anglican educational institutions and ideals began to reflect the
influence of Jewish learning—an influence far greater than the
number of Jews in the society would seem to promise. The Jews'
self-defensive wit and dramatic heritage was first expressed in
the Yiddish theater, then worked its way into American show
business from all directions—entrepreneurial, artistic. Thus the
American sense of humor itself was colored with the traditions of
a people homeless for hundreds of generations, home in America
at last.

The Italians were not necessarily outcasts in their own land;
nor were they religious "aliens" in the United States; but much
about their culture made them, perhaps, slower to assimilate

The movement for
woman's suffrage in the United
States may be said to have begun
in July 1848, when the first
woman's rights convention in
history met in Seneca Falls, New
York. The movement grew steadily
in the second half of the nineteenth century. By 1913 twelve
states had granted women the vote.
That year an independent organization, which later adopted the
name National Woman's Party,
resolved to use the voting power of
the women in these states to secure
a federal amendment. The organization met with strong opposition
from many politicians, who were
wary of it as a force for reform.
During World War I, however, the
women's contribution to man-
power-drained America helped
advance their cause, and in 1920
the Nineteenth Amendment became part of the Constitution.

110

than some of the earlier immigrant groups. Italy, like Ireland and Germany, was for many a worn-out nation in the nineteenth century: the soil seemed to be used up, and persisting land-distribution practices frustrated youth, who looked forward to little but hardship in the future. All told, some five million Italians migrated to the United States, more than any other latter-day immigrant group except the Germans. Their strong sense of family and communal tradition survived in America, whether they settled in the wine country of California or the Italian sector of a big city.

As time passed, the Italian-Americans' political influence began to have a profound effect on the nation's local governments: next to the Irish, the Italians have probably produced more mayors, county executives, and city councilmen than any other ethnic group. Inheritors of an almost feudal tradition, in which the local precinct more or less governed itself, the Italians brought their skill at managing local affairs in a decentralized system to the United States, especially at the municipal and statewide level. The Italians also brought to America their ancient heritage of music and art. Here again, the influence of an immigrant group—in this case on American music and painting and drama—has been disproportionately great. And of course Italian food has become as American as apple pie—*more* American; for in the past decade, pizza has become the American people's prized snack.

The Chinese families that began to arrive on the Pacific coast midway through the nineteenth century arrived for the same reason that Americans of European stock headed westward to the same ocean: gold. The fact that they came at all is remarkable. The Chinese family, more than that of any other immigrant group, is a tightly woven unit, woven not only member-to-member, but member-to-ancestors, ancestors-to-land. Moreover, China was such a poor and overpopulated nation in the 1800s that the struggle for existence occupied almost every waking hour. With their close ties to family, home, and land, and with all their time occupied, the Chinese had little chance of hearing about the outside world, much less of being drawn to it. All the same, gold is a powerful substance. It not only makes men rich when they find it; it also seems to contain its own broadcast system, and its own magnetic power. After gold was discovered in California in 1848 and 1849, seamen carried the news to every port on earth. From the ports of China—particularly in Kwangtung Province near Canton and Hong Kong, where the foreign ships docked—the news spread. To evaluate the effect—and the scale—of the rumors we need only look at the Chinese nickname for America in the second half of the nineteenth century: *Gum Shan*, "Mountain of Gold." Within thirty years some one hundred thousand Chinese crossed the great ocean, searching for the magic rocks of riches. Few found gold, but the Chinese found other sources of livelihood.

Even more than the toil-hardened European immigrants, the Chinese knew how to work. When they arrived in California, the more practical among them realized promptly that the chance of their finding gold was small. (Even then, the Chinese had less opportunity to prospect, because discrimination against them was a handicap. They could not always find lodging or camp with the white-skinned prospectors in mining camps, and in some areas they were not even able to purchase tools.) Being practical, however, the newcomers did see a way to earn enough money to buy passage back to China. Unlike the American prospectors, they were not "home." Frozen out of most jobs, they took work that no other men would do. In camp after camp Chinese cooks began preparing meals; fellow immigrants got themselves soap, scrubboards, and irons, and went from camp to camp doing laundry. Before long the Oriental newcomers abandoned their original plans to earn just enough money to buy return passage.

At some unknown California camp, the first permanent Chinese contribution to American society was developed. Combining their own food traditions with the needs of serving a big crowd, the Chinese cooks invented a strictly American, Chinese-

The capitols in New York and Philadelphia were headquarters for the federal government until 1800. In that year, during the administration of John Adams, the government offices and departments moved to the new city of Washington, D.C.

113

style stew: served with noodles it was chow mein; without, chop suey.

During the Civil War, work continued on the Central Pacific and Union Pacific Railroads, but the war itself—which caused a slowdown in immigrant arrivals—both increased the need for workers and reduced their availability. Desperate, the railroads' directors approached a Chinese recruiting agency known as the Six Companies and asked for help. The Six Companies rounded up thousands of willing workers, who were glad to earn the modest thirty-five dollars a month pay. A rebellion in China during the early 1860s helped provide workers, too. So as the (predominantly) Irish laborers laid rails westward, the Chinese laid rails eastward. (Of the ten thousand men who built the railroads on the western side, nine thousand were Chinese.) When the rails were joined in 1869, the Chinese were suddenly unemployed, but they managed to get other jobs, jobs that were too trying for most Americans.

Anti-Chinese agitation reached epidemic proportions after the Panic of 1873, and the depression that followed ended the prosperity of California and threw thousands of men throughout the West out of work. So great was the prejudice against the Chinese that many Chinese immigrants returned to Asia. Furthermore, an act of Congress in 1882 barred Chinese immigration for ten years—and even more restrictive legislation was passed later. Nevertheless, the remaining Chinese—particularly those who had prospered in the laundry and restaurant businesses—quietly put down roots in American cities.

Oddly enough, the anti-Chinese legislation of the late nineteenth century backfired. Faced with a manpower shortage, many American growers in California now found themselves wishing there were more cheap Chinese labor. In the face of the restrictions, the growers began importing Japanese workers. The Japanese, most of whom remained in California, proved to be as enterprising as the Chinese. In 1920, for example, the Japanese comprised only 2 percent of the state's population. But they produced 13 percent of the state's agricultural product.

Through much of the nineteenth century, and well into the twentieth, immigrants had come from Europe. Less well remembered is the migration from Canada. Almost a million Canadians crossed the border: French Canadians came to work in New England's mills; Ontario's emigrants favored the industrial cities south of the Great Lakes. Immigrants from Canada, especially those speaking English, adjusted to American life with little difficulty.

A law enacted in 1965 made it much easier for immigrants south of the border to enter the United States. Several hundred thousand Mexicans had entered legally before that law was passed. More continued to arrive, legally and illegally. Those entering illegally were often smuggled in by labor contractors. Most of these immigrants found their way to California, Arizona, and Texas, where they harvested vegetables, fruits, sugar cane, and cotton. Off the farms, Mexicans in the 1950s supplied half of the total number of railroad-track laborers west of Chicago. The West Indies sent about 300,000 by 1930, most of them from the British West Indies.

It was from Puerto Rico, after World War II, that immigrants came to the mainland in large numbers. An overcrowded island had promised them a bleak future. Most of them settled in New York City, which by 1960 had a Puerto Rican population of over 600,000.

They found jobs, as others had before them, requiring little or no skills. They became orderlies in hospitals, worked in hotels and restaurants. As they learned English, they became sales clerks or got jobs in the garment industry, once dominated by Jews and Italians.

America's reputation as an "asylum for the oppressed" was put to the test with the rise of fascism and communism in the twentieth century. Fleeing Nazi Germany and fascist Italy, many thousands of well-educated, skilled men and women arrived in America. From Soviet Russia and the countries she subjugated, especially Hungary, more thousands sought sanctuary in the United States. They were joined by the many thousands who fled Castro's Cuba. Miami became the Mecca for most of them; their industriousness transformed that city's economy. In the mid-1970s, another refugee group, the South Vietnamese—over 100,000—flew to safety in the United States.

It almost goes without saying that the role of black Americans in the formation of American society differed from that of all other immigrant peoples. The Africans who were brought to this continent soon after its discovery by Europeans and who continued to be brought until 1808 (and illegally thereafter) did not migrate of their own free will; they were slaves when they got here, and even after emancipation their participation in the civic processes of the United States was in varying degrees regulated by societal and legislative forces. In the overall development of the American people, however, the Afro-Americans were in a profound way the most influential of all hyphenated Americans.

The most cursory thumbing-through of the pages of an American-history text reveals how thoroughly the presence of the Afro-American in the New World is woven into the warp and woof of this country. His presence affected the debates of the Constitution framers, and the major legislation and most of the greatest debates of the nation's first seven decades were directly or indirectly concerned with him. The Missouri Compromise, the Kansas-Nebraska Act, the Dred Scott Decision, the admission of virtually all new states after the first thirteen, and countless other landmarks in American history reflected the "peculiar institution" constructed around him. That institution was the primary cause of the Civil War. Reconstruction gave the black American citizenship and rights; the Ku Klux Klan was formed to deny them to him; Reconstruction was ended at his expense. Thereafter scarcely a decade passed without a race-related issue; civil rights was the cause that lasted a century. Thus the black American has never been far from the consciousness of white Americans. Naturally, any such person cannot help but exercise considerable influence over the development of a national consciousness—and a national consciousness, after all, is the common denominator of a people.

And then there is the direct influence. By the time of emancipation, the African origins of black Americans were recalled only in general terms, seldom in specific ones. Denied the ethnic-preservation institutions of other immigrants, the black Americans could keep no records; most had no idea which tribe they had belonged to, which African traditions they had brought with them. The one certainty was that they did in fact bring some. Their speech was accented with cadences of forgotten tongues; their work songs retained the harmonies and rhythms of certain but unidentifiable musical legacies. And the African traditions, altered and Americanized through generations of bondage, began to work their way into an evolving American set of traditions well before the War Between the States.

The most obvious and justifiably celebrated influence was through music. Slaves who were not taught to write could not continue whatever literary traditions their ancestry might have contained; slaves without a society of their own to build monuments to and without the materials necessary for the creation of art were in no position to pass architectural or sculptural traditions on to their offspring. But the slaves sang; they sang of their burdensome lot; they sang of their struggle; and it must be assumed that their songs did embody the African legacy. Stephen Foster was the first celebrated, but not the first white, American to appreciate and incorporate the sophistication of that legacy into American music. Emancipated, black Americans continued to add musical modules to their sad musical structure; work ballads evolved into the blues; their vital instrumental music—at first made with improvised instruments—evolved into jazz. Blues and jazz have had a profound influence on the course of American popular and serious music. The genealogy is complex: from one form of blues came the white singer's handling of popular songs: patronizingly, the turn-of-the-century singers even put blackfaces on to sing, as if to acknowledge that their "Toot-toot-Toot-sies" and "Makin' Whoopies" were not entirely their own. From jazz came the rhythms and harmonies that characterized the most American works of the most American serious composers: Gershwin, Copland, Bernstein. (Long before, in the middle of the nineteenth century, Louis M. Gottschalk composed music that had some of the flavor of these composers.) So pronounced was the black presence in American music that even foreign composers, trained in the most conservative traditions of European music, were immediately struck by it when they visited this country, and the black influence worked its way back across the Atlantic, in the scores of Dvořák, Ravel, and others. Further evolution produced the sophisticated jazz of the 1930s and succeeding two decades, and, through swing, the more conventional music of the dance palace, the Broadway stage, the motion picture. Another line went from blues to rhythm-and-blues, to rock-and-roll, which was an international music. Thus the evolutionary process crossed the Atlantic, was altered by the Beatles, Rolling Stones, and others, and then came back again to these shores.

But the main influence of black Americans on the development of a national American character has been effected through the black experience itself. Black Americans have had a different life in the United States from white Americans, and their experience has been as much a part of American history as any other immigrant experience. The realization that that experience has shaped us, white and black, has only recently come to all Americans. The results of the realization are startling. As we approach the two-hundredth birthday of our country, we have begun to assimilate the black experience into our national character—not merely through our music, not merely through the black-American slang that has become national jargon, but through the understanding that we are all Americans, and that whatever one hyphenated group has experienced, we have all experienced.

THE MAKING OF A SOCIETY

FOLDOUT PAGE—

4.

THE MAKING OF
A SOCIETY

HOWEVER DIVERSE THEIR ORIGINS, the Americans who populated the young country had essentially uniform aspirations: they wished to live in freedom, with a reasonable degree of material comfort, and they wished to go as far as their ambition, talent, diligence, and intelligence could take them. And for the most part American society was cooperative. It provided the opportunities, pointed the way, and gave all comers their choice. The way was eased by public education, which was compulsory on the lower level, and beyond that there were state universities. In the nineteenth century, only a small proportion of Americans went on to higher education, but in following years the number grew large. In the schools that younger immigrants entered, they learned of American heroes, Washington and Lincoln, who supplanted the idols of Old World families. In little red schoolhouses or in more imposing buildings a diverse people came to share a heritage to be passed on to later generations.

The pace of life in America was faster than in Europe. Visitors noted that in cities, especially, eating was "gobble, gulp, and go." "Time is money," the immigrant heard. Faster communications knit a vast country closer together. Less than a half century before that golden spike joined the railroad tracks at Promontory Point, Utah, in 1869, it might easily have taken a week to travel from Washington to Philadelphia by coach. Now, in the same time, a traveler could go from New York to San Francisco, nearly three thousand miles away. And not only the traveler, but goods, newspapers, candidates for national political office, confections, fashions. Twenty years earlier a New England textile manufacturer could stay in business manufacturing, say, organdy dress-material. If organdy was fashionable in New York in a given year, it wouldn't be stylish in Baltimore until three or four years later; then it would move on down to Richmond, then to Atlanta and New Orleans, then up to Kansas City—all this taking years—and then across the country to the West Coast. Then came the train. With the train came profitable mail-order merchandising, and the traveling salesman, and catalogues. Suddenly the woman in Seattle and the woman in Norfolk were turning the same pages of the same Sears catalogue in the same month—and ordering organdy. Mills in New England had to anticipate nationwide fash-

ions and nationwide changes of fashion to be ready when Sears placed its order.

Then, too, the train brought to Americans an institution—or a conglomeration of institutions—that would have an astonishing effect on the development of American society. Americans, along with most people, have always liked to be entertained. They have enjoyed the theater, the dance-hall show, and even the political debate, which was invariably well-attended in the nineteenth century. The train made it possible for entertainers to

In the nineteenth century, railroads and rivers were the main arteries of a circulatory system through which ideas and fashions flowed as smoothly as cargo, joining the nation's parts and forging a whole as conclusively as events and legislation. In the twentieth century, automobiles and airplanes have made the system at once more complex and tighter. Only a couple of generations ago, most Americans spent their lives within a relatively small area; today people routinely fly from coast to coast. The world and indeed the universe have been shrinking, and now, thanks to the rocket ship, humankind stands on the threshold of a new age.

travel about much more extensively than before. By the 1880s, enterprising promoters in New York had developed a well-organized system to get entertainment to a maximum number of people across the country. This was the vaudeville "circuit" system. The very best New York shows were sent on the road on the "first circuit"—which included the finest theaters in the biggest cities around the country. The second circuit included a few more cities, perhaps slightly less grand theaters, and entertainment just a trifle less polished. Promising acts were sent around the fourth or fifth circuit, which hit a few small towns, and acts on the way down were sent on circuits that made hundreds of stops in towns, mining camps, and wherever else an audience could be assembled at a quarter a head. Though the quality of entertainment on the vaudeville circuits ranged from superb to awful, "show business" contributed a great deal to the unification of Americans. National

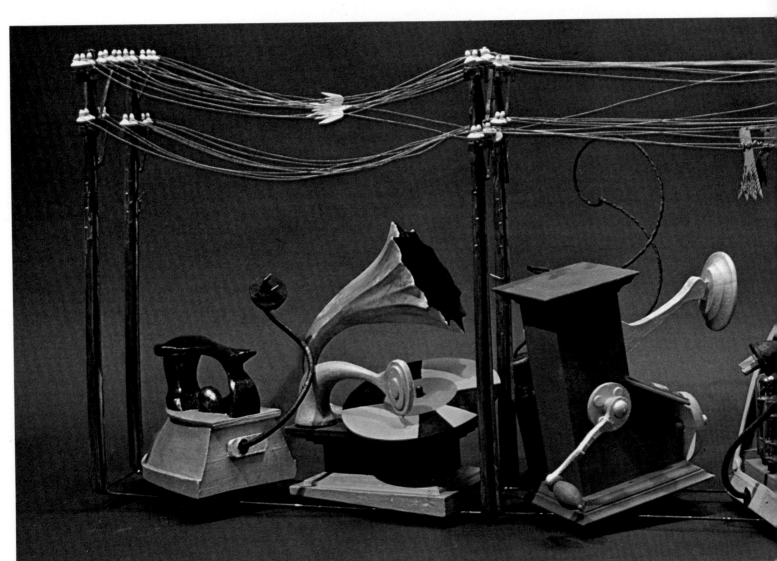

issues, national concerns became nationally discussed—even if the source of discussion was a vaudeville clown's poor jokes, or a temperance play. And—after the turn of the century in particular—entertainment gave the nation its first nonpolitical celebrities. Every boy wanted to be as strong as Sandow the Magnificent, every girl as sweet and wistful as Maude Adams as Peter Pan.

Even more than transportation, communications media have made America a whole nation. The record player and motion pictures, developed as devices for entertainment, transcended mere pleasure-giving; they exposed Americans to the music, manners, and morals that other Americans were creating—and they did so instantly. The radio's effect was even greater: it, too, entertained, but it also made news instant news; it gave people the opportunity to follow events as they happened, to share the events, to listen to the president's voice at the moment of crisis. Television completed the process: national issues were brought home to every American. And when people wanted to discuss the events with one another—or just say hello—they had at their fingertips the most personal and intimate of all communications devices, the telephone.

In 1889, Thomas Edison—whose contribution to the development of American society is well known—invented the Kinetoscope, which within ten years evolved into the magic lantern: motion pictures. By 1910 trains were carrying cans containing reels of film to every nook and cranny of the nation: now girls curled their hair like Mary Pickford, boys practiced their fast-draw to be as fast as Bronco Billy, and everybody—but *everybody*—started laughing at the antics of a comical tramp played by a shy Englishman named Charlie Chaplin. Edison also produced the phonograph, and suddenly the songs sung by the traveling vaude-villians could be heard in record stores in Portland, Oregon, and Portland, Maine. "I'm Only a Bird in a Gilded Cage," sang the

Sports provide Americans with one of the last large-scale entertainments that stress not the national whole but regional boosterism. What better way to bask in local pride than to have the state university win the Orange Bowl, or the local team win the World Series. Still, transportation and communication have made even regional heroes nationally recognized. O. J. Simpson and Hank Aaron are national, not local, heroes.

folks in San Diego and Boston, while their upstairs neighbors tried to drown them out with "After the Ball Is Over." A people who see the same shows, admire the same celebrities, escape to the same movies, sing the same songs, laugh at the same jokes are in the last analysis one people—whatever their accents, wherever their origins, whatever their individual aspirations.

Americans were already one people early in the century, and yet the unifying devices were nothing then compared with what was to come. The motion picture industry was a huge industry by the end of World War I; Hollywood set fashions and recharted the course of American manners for two generations. No matter that the taste-makers were foreign-born men with names like Lubitsch and Von Stroheim and Goldfish (who later became Goldwyn); they were all part of Hollywood. You never knew where your heroes were going to come from in the twenties: today it was Babe Ruth, out of a Baltimore orphanage, but tomorrow it might be Rudolph Valentino, Italian-born, playing to an audience many times larger than the Babe's. At the same time the crystal set evolved into the radio, and the popular songs of the phonograph records reached an even greater audience—reached into virtually every American home; and while downstairs in Newport, Rhode Island, and Santa Barbara, California, Dad took a shower singing "Button Up Your Overcoat," Mom upstairs tried "Tip-toe Through the Tulips." Paul Whiteman's music was all the rage, but another favorite was Greta Garbo, the beautiful movie star whose English was heavily accented with her Scandinavian tongue.

No teenager who valued friendship would venture to a dance without learning the Bunny Hop, the Charleston, and the Turkey Trot; the kids knew all the words to the latest songs; college kids dressed alike and talked the same slang and listened to jazz and during Prohibition sipped bootleg whiskey from straws stuck in bottles stuck in pockets of raccoon coats.

Information and entertainment were broadcast over the radio, projected in the movies, and promoted in magazines. Advertising told Americans pointedly what show business told Americans by dramatic example—that they had better know what was the latest, that how they would be judged by others depended on how they presented themselves. The automobile had been an early success in twentieth-century America; the appearance of the Model T Ford in 1908 had made the car accessible to the working man. But the car as transportation was not all the car was to be. In the twenties and thirties, and even more after World War II, the car became an expression of the owner, indeed an extension of him. No swinging bachelor drove a black Chevy; no settled family man bought a Stutz Bearcat. But family man and bachelor alike picked up the information that the times were presenting: that having the latest car was as important as having a car.

The Great Depression and World War II slowed the development of certain aspects of American society, but they contributed mightily to others. With no money to go out, Americans stayed in and listened to the radio. So more national celebrities

were created: Jack Benny, Amos 'n' Andy, Bing Crosby, and—oh, yes—President Franklin D. Roosevelt, who used the wonderful little box to talk straight talk to Americans right in their own living rooms. The theater and the vaudeville circuits had hard times, but movies—because tickets were cheap—thrived—and talked, too. Girls were as snooty as Katharine Hepburn or as down-to-earth as Joan Blondell or as zany as Carole Lombard or as smart as Jean Arthur; boys were as tough as James Cagney, as cocky as Clark Gable, as likable as Jimmy Stewart or as strong-and-silent as Gary Cooper. Popular songs either acknowledged the Great Depression—"Brother, Can You Spare a Dime?"—or thumbed noses at it—"We're in the money, the skies are sunny, Old Man Depression, you are through, you done us wrong."

After World War II, the automobile continued to shape the growth of cities and suburbs, and radio and the movies were replaced by television. The coasts that were a week apart when the gold spike was hammered home were hours apart before long. The Brooklyn Dodgers moved to Los Angeles, the New York Giants to San Francisco, the professional sporting world expanded to and through every corner of the nation. The boundaries of the nation seemed to shrink. A pair of double arches identified the kind of hamburger you could get in Connecticut and Iowa and Arizona; the same bucket of fried chicken turned electrically over highways from New Hampshire to New Mexico.

No birthday party is complete without refreshments, and Americans celebrating the two-hundredth birthday of their country will no doubt enjoy appropriate snacks and feasts. In Boston families may go out for some Kentucky fried chicken; Maine lobster stuffed with Chesapeake Bay crabmeat may be the day's special at a fine Los Angeles restaurant; New York corned-beef sandwiches will be ordered in Kansas City. And then of course, in addition to peanuts and popcorn, plenty of other traditional "American" foods will be consumed, among them bagels and pizza.

Telephone calls from the Atlantic to the Pacific cost pennies; the same news is carried the same night in Philadelphia and Spokane. A political candidate may be made or broken by the image he or she projects on T.V.

Everything is the same, you hear it said; we have lost or are losing the differences between us. And yet, if we compare the entertainment we get today with the entertainment we got, say, twenty years ago, we'll come up with a very different kind of information. In the 1950s, the American television family—that is, the typical American family, as television liked to show it—was middle class, suburban, harmonious, and always worked things out. It was in fact an artificial family, not an average one. But in this our two-hundredth year, what sort of American family do we see when we turn on the T.V.? We see Archie Bunker and his radical son-in-law; we see the Jeffersons, black and prosperous; we see Sanford and Son, black and poor; we see a Jewish New York window dresser and her Irish building-wrecker husband; we see odd couples and big singing families; families with roots in every culture on earth; families with liberal politics and conservative politics; families of different colors; families working out problems, and families not working out all problems but loving each other anyway; American families. Which one is really typical?

They all are; that they are is America's greatest achievement, and the best possible reason to celebrate a birthday. The bond that unites them all is the conviction that they must preserve their democratic heritage.

INDEX

All numbers refer to pages. Numbers in *italic* type refer to picture captions.